# MOBILE COMMERCE 2.0

## WHERE PAYMENTS, LOCATION AND ADVERTISING CONVERGE

Majeed Ahmad

**SMARTPHONE CHRONICLE**

This publication is designed to provide accurate and authoritative information in regard to the subject matter covered. It is sold with the understanding that the publisher is not engaged in rendering professional services. The advice and strategies contained herein may not be suitable for your situation. You should consult with a professional where appropriate. Neither the publisher nor author shall be liable for any loss of profit or any other commercial damages, including but not limited to special, incidental, consequential, or other damages.

A prior and smaller version of this book has been published on Amazon Kindle under the title "Business Untethered: Smartphone and the Revival of Mobile Commerce" on October 24, 2012.

ISBN-10: 1484144929
ISBN-13: 9781484144923
Library of Congress Control Number: 2013907873
CreateSpace Independent Publishing Platform
North Charleston, South Carolina

# CONTENTS

# PROLOGUE

*"The cell phone is the single most transformative technology for development."*

— Jeffrey Sachs, Columbia University economist and emerging markets expert

Jack Dorsey grew up in downtown St. Louis and was obsessed with city life, the flow of human interaction, and computer programming. He had always kept a journal and had pondered on how technology could make human tasks easier. Dorsey was working as a programmer in San Francisco when RIM's mobile e-mail device started making waves in the late 1990s. He instantly got hooked on the BlackBerry and wrote a piece of software to categorize the e-mails as journal entries. Dorsey was also an early user of LiveJournal, a social network that let people see friends' posts about their activities in reverse chronological order. He had been writing rudimentary software programs for dispatching taxis, ambulances and courier services since his high school days. So here, at the crossroads of BlackBerry and LiveJournal, he thought he could do for himself what he had been doing for years in helping taxis and couriers: declare where he was and what he was doing.

One night in July 2000, Dorsey wrote a code that enabled him to have an e-mail re-posted to as many people as he wanted. He entered the e-mail addresses of five friends into the software, wrote an e-mail with subject line "I'm at the Bison Paddock watching the bison" and took a walk to Golden Gate Park. His friends weren't terribly enthused because no one else had a mobile e-mail device. Moreover, no one really cared what Dorsey was doing in the park. But he kept refining the concept, and by 2001, he had sketched out a basic template for a service he termed as Stat.us. A few years later, in 2006, Dorsey joined the San Francisco software startup Odeo which was aiming to produce a directory of podcasts. But when Apple incorporated a directory of podcasts into iTunes, Odeo's business plan was thrown out of the window. At that time, with Odeo in full reset mode, its boss Evan Williams asked his staff for new ideas, and Dorsey laid out his vision for Stat.us.

Dorsey was passionate about city life—and locomotives, police cars and taxicabs that were part of it. He was fascinated by the way drivers and dispatchers succinctly conveyed locations by radio in taxicab communications. Dorsey proposed that Odeo create a service that would allow anyone to write a line or two and send that message to anyone who wanted to receive it. The short text alert was a way to add a missing human element in the ever-expanding digital life. Timing was impeccable because text messaging had just begun to take off in the United States. Dorsey would work closely with several others on a project called "twttr." Before long, the team had a working product, and Dorsey authored the first tweet "just setting up my twttr" for co-workers. Williams wanted to turn Odeo into an incubator for multiple businesses, so Dorsey was made CEO of the new venture that became known to the world as Twitter. By 2011, when Twitter, with its precision and minimalism, had become central to modern culture, Dorsey had 1.6 million followers.

However, by the time Twitter became a cultural force, Dorsey was being pushed out the door. Though he was made chairman, he was no longer an employee in the company. He had seen this all before during the dotcom frenzy when in 1998 he, along with Greg Kidd, had set up dNet service for dispatching couriers online. They raised money, hired a CEO, and then the new boss pushed the co-founders out over strategy disagreements just when the tech bubble burst. Fast forward to October 16, 2008, Evan Williams took over the role of CEO at Twitter and the episode was like déjà vu. But before Dorsey had time to sink into despondency, he got a call from Jim McKelvey. McKelvey had hired Dorsey as a teenage programmer for his St. Louis–based company that archived documents onto CD-ROMs; he later became Dorsey's business partner. Later in 2008, McKelvey passed on the reins of his software firm and set up a glassblowing studio in St. Louis. One day, after losing a customer of US$2,000 just because he wasn't equipped to accept the American Express card, he called Dorsey.

They were talking on their iPhones when McKelvey proposed to build a system that would make and accept credit-card payments on smartphones. Within days McKelvey left St. Louis, moved to San Francisco to team up with Dorsey and Tristan O'Tierney, and started working on what would eventually become Square Inc. It took them a month to cobble together a working prototype codenamed Squirrel. Dorsey worked on the back-end server, O'Tierney on the iPhone app and McKelvey worked on the hardware and on establishing relationships with payment partners. McKelvey eventually built the prototype credit card reader; otherwise, he didn't actually work at Square on regular basis. In 2009, the three conceived a business around a free device that would be dispensed to anyone who signed up: a tiny, square-shaped credit-card reader that could be plugged into the headphone jack of an iPhone, Android phone, or tablet computer.

The idea of Square came to market in early 2010 with a very compelling value proposition: give everyone the chance to process credit card transactions. When a credit or a debit card was swiped through a small magnetic card reader hooked onto a smartphone, it read the data and converted it into an audio signal. The handset microphone picked up the audio and routed it to Square's app on the phone. From there the encrypted data was transmitted using either Wi-Fi or a 3G Internet connection to back-end severs, which in turn, communicated with the payment networks to complete the transactions.

Square helped fuel interest in mobile payments by turning the iPhone into a cash register with this matchbook-sized credit card reader that plugged into the iPhone and automated the entire process. Customers swiped their credit card onto the phone-attached card reader, signed the phone touchscreen with a finger or stylus, and got an e-mail or a text with a receipt. After the payment was processed, money was deposited into merchant's bank account. Square's customers included food trucks, hairdressers, small retailers, restaurants, and taxicabs, and the service lured them due to its simple software and its flat 2.75 percent transaction fee. In 2012, Square claimed it was already processing more than US$10 billion in payments a year, and that some three million merchants were using its service.

The initial goals of Square were rather modest: help small businesses and individual merchants who were cut out of the mainstream payments business due to their inability to accept credit cards. As merchants started taking more and more payments, they became more confident and more sophisticated about what features they needed, and they started asking Square for more tools. The iPad was just emerging on the scene, providing more real estate than the iPhone, and that got Square thinking about providing a complete point-of-sale (POS) solution rather than simply a reader for small businesses and individuals. Dorsey saw an opportunity to revamp the whole payment experience. So, Square began giving small vendors the tools to make intelligent decisions with the same sort of inventory management, sales data, and analytics that their larger competitors had already been enjoying.

For mobile users, Square launched Pay with Square, previously known as Card Case, which people carried on their phones; it allowed them to track their entire shopping history as well as build loyalty with stores. Open the case, take out the card and there would be a list of everything a mobile user had bought from a particular vendor. Pay with Square was also the upstart's customer-focused app for iOS and Android that allowed mobile users to pay handsfree at Square-enabled merchants and provided them the ability to discover nearby Square merchants. When mobile users walked into a store, they could simply give their name at the register and the merchant could perform a seamless transaction without the customer ever having to pull out a phone. Besides convenience, it helped establish a subconscious emotional connection between the merchant and the customer. The apps like Pay with Square manifested the company's vision of one-click shopping experience for the real world.

Mobile consumers, using GPS and Google Maps on their handsets, could see where the nearest Square-powered merchants were located. When they tapped on one of those merchants, they could also see relevant information like hours of operation, menus, specials, coupons, comments, and more. Square was geared toward merchant discovery with an almost artistic approach to commerce. The geofencing-enabled app also added social elements to the customer-merchant interaction. A mobile user could tweet about a merchant on Twitter, text message details about the merchant, or e-mail a link about the merchant. That way a mobile user could mark specific merchants for future reference. Facebook sharing functionality would be next. With this wealth of information, the upstart's Pay with Square for mobile phone users and Register software for merchants could make an even greater impact than the initial payment processing product had made.

Square Register, the company's iPad business app, kicked off with a very simple reward system, but eventually it added information for business owners on how much a user had purchased, giving them the option of choosing when to surprise their customer with a loyalty gift. Square's enhanced loyalty and rewards system, which allowed merchants to create digital punch cards for users, rewarded them for their first visit and continued patronage. Mobile users would be able to get a punch card in their Pay with Square mobile app for each purchase and could chart their progress toward their next reward. On the other hand, merchants could get users in the door by providing a percentage discount or a free item with their first purchase. And for regular customers, they could reward a set number of visits or total spend. A fully automated system helped the merchant in two ways: it eliminated the act of having to tailor a specific deal at the point of sale, and it played on the consumer's desire to earn VIP-like deals.

Square's tools for merchants laid the groundwork for deeper customer-merchant relationships. With Square Register, a point-of-sale system designed for the iPad, merchants would be able to get better analytics on sales with item-level reporting broken down by hours and time of day or week. Businesses could also see how sales were doing by employee shift. Inventory management features enabled merchants to easily create categories of items, making it easier to handle greater quantities of products. The iPad-based Register app also offered easier discounting of products, so merchants could set a percentage or dollar discount on any item. Collectively, the Pay with Square and Register features further bridged the gap between merchant and customer within the Square ecosystem. These features embodied a shift that could potentially change how consumers viewed their interactions with merchants, from a mechanical transaction to a running dialogue, in which the merchant could clue in the consumer on everything from the day's deals to whether or not their favorite item was currently available.

Over the past decades, there had been a wholesale destruction of mom-and-pop shops as small businesses watched customers flee and take their business to large retail chains. It wasn't just that they couldn't compete on price; it was that they were unable to compete against sophisticated inventory management. Things cost more not just because small businesses didn't have the scale to purchase at the same volume as large chain stores, but also because for many of them inventory management was expensive and inefficient. Square's Register software was looking to change that. The startup was seeking to democratize business intelligence, allowing anyone to set up a point-of-sale offering without having to make a huge upfront investment. It was creating a level playing field for the little guy, who otherwise couldn't afford the kind of business analytics that large retailers took for granted.

In August 2012, Square announced a deal with Starbucks to make it possible to pay with Square's app in 7,000 Starbucks stores. Using the Square Wallet was similar to the Starbucks app in that customers tapped "pay here" and scanned a QR code to pay. Mobile users had to connect a credit or debit card to the app for the first time, but once they did, payments were automatically authorized. Next, in July 2013, the Silicon Valley mobile payments upstart came up with the idea of Square Stand, a piece of hardware that helped turn an iPad into an upright point-of-sale device. In addition to docking an iPad, it included a card swipe function for taking payments. Square was also making available third-party accessories, including cash drawers, receipt printers and barcode scanners.

By 2012, Square was processing 11 million mobile payments a day. If Twitter helped transform communications and social life across the globe, Square was another game changer that created a brand new payment system for everyday transactions by marrying the convenience of plastic and mobility. Both Twitter and Square were essentially communication technologies. While Twitter made anyone a broadcaster or newsmaker, Square offered everyone the opportunity to become a merchant. Jack Dorsey was the pioneering spirit behind these great technological breakthroughs of the smartphone era, and he drew part of his inspiration from another great innovator of his time: Steve Jobs. Much like Jobs, Dorsey tended to view himself more of a craftsman than an entrepreneur or a technologist, and like Jobs, he produced an integrated system in the Square payment network whereas others mostly assembled clumsy agglomerations.

The prologue highlighted Dorsey's Square because real leaders in the mobile payments realm were small upstarts like Square. They were bringing a tremendous amount of innovation to this nascent industry by thinking about it from the ground up. A closer look at Dorsey's innovations reveals that as the smartphone was coming of age, communications technology was constantly colliding and converging with social and economic realms. The essence of this phenomenon was sheer simplicity and democratization of information for the benefit of common man, a process that kick-started with the advent of the Internet more than a decade ago. This book attempts to explore this confluence of mobile communications with social and economic domains and develop a clearer picture of the prodigy commonly called mobile commerce or m-commerce for short.

Mobile commerce—the digital sales channel of the future—embodied the adoption of next-generation mobile shopping, payment, and ad infrastructures. It was defined as the delivery of trusted transaction services over mobile devices for the exchange of goods and services between consumers, merchants and financial institutions. In fact, it encompassed any commerce transaction that used mobile devices like smartphones and tablets over a wireless network. A mobile device could be an initiator or a consumer of a commerce transaction and the entire transaction didn't need to happen on the mobile device; some part of the processing could be on stationary systems like computer servers and other hosting services.

Mobile commerce enabled users to access the net—and thus a plethora of buying and selling opportunities—without needing to find a place to plug in. So commerce using mobile devices extended way beyond the traditional e-commerce norms. The book addresses that very premise and delves into the technical, economical and application frameworks of mobile commerce to provide readers with the bigger picture and identify opportunities in the next big thing of the mobile juggernaut. Here we go!

# 1 FIRST, THE VISION

*"Mobile commerce is going to be the most fantastic thing that a time-starved world has ever seen."*

— Jeff Bezos, founder and CEO of Amazon.com, quoted in an Associated Press article in March 2000

In 2007, soon after Olli-Pekka Kallasvuo took charge of Nokia as the new CEO, he embarked on an ambitious technology acquisition. Nokia bought the Chicago–based digital map company Navteq Corp. for hefty US$8.1 billion to bring navigation out of car and deliver it to pedestrians. Nokia coined the buzzword "context-aware Internet" while asserting that it would reshape the Internet. To accomplish that Internet panacea, the Finnish mobile phone giant was pinning its hopes on operator-independent, cross-platform phones conceived through the development of new software and services.

The Finnish wireless bellwether claimed that Map 2.0 would enable context-aware Internet by combining multimedia features with the freewheeling Internet and assisted-GPS technology.

Nokia engineers claimed that by adding context—such as time, place, and people—to the Internet, the mobile web experience would become something entirely different. Once the context was added to the network, they contended, the Internet experience would become more mobile, contextual, and personal than on the desktop. The building blocks necessary to make this happen included GPS, broadband access, a back-end service, and enough processing power and memory residing on mobile phones. Here is one scenario depicting how it would actually work: a user takes pictures with a camera phone and the GPS coordinates are simultaneously stored in a metadata file; Bluetooth could sniff around and discover who is around him or her. Location, therefore, would no longer be an application; it would become a core fabric of the mobile Internet.

Nokia managers loved to play up fascinating new scenarios at technology press events. Their hyperbole was reminiscent to the early days of mobile commerce talk, which was stimulated by the arrival of Wireless Application Protocol (WAP)-based mobile phones. At that time, during early 2000s, marketing dream weavers conjured up whiz-bang scenarios in which mobile-phone users would resort to all kinds of amazing adventures. One might have heard this: walking down the street, a user approaches a Starbucks coffeehouse and his or her mobile phone starts ringing; on the handset screen pops up a coupon for a $1 latte. Or this: A user strides into a department store and slips into that perfect pair of jeans. A bit pricey! No sweat for his or her mobile phone. The user punches the bar code of the jeans into his or her handset and receives 20 percent discount from an online retailer.

But all these pie-in-the-sky ideas ended up as wishful thinking; broadcasting people every time they passed a McDonald or a Starbucks seemed incredibly unrealistic at that time. What Nokia did in 2007 was recycle this notion by combining two chic technologies of the time—the mobile web and GPS-based location—and started spreading the context-aware Internet gospel. However, after three years and some failed projects, there was little evidence of any tangible payback to Nokia's foray into location-centric premium phones. When the dust settled, Nokia seemed to have fallen to the classical marketing paradox that was all too familiar in the twilight world of the mobile phone and the Internet.

Apple, in a stark contrast to Nokia, carefully rationalized the supporting technology components, worked out a robust product roadmap, and then mobilized its legendary marketing machine. It's official now that the iPhone was initially conceived as a phone that would play music and video from iTunes, but its primary appeal quickly became the millions of head-slapping, useful software applications that ran on it. The iPhone certainly played music, but owners were just as likely to use it to check the weather, book dinner reservations, read a newspaper, get directions, or play a quick game of Taxiball on the subway. The creation of the App Store for the iPhone was a revolution that literally changed the smartphone world overnight and helped the iPhone reach dizzying heights.

The Cupertino, California–based company sent shockwaves across the wireless world by readily shifting the consumer expectations for smartphones. The App Store created billions of dollars in new revenue for software makers and catapulted the iPhone into being the largest must-have device on the planet. Suddenly the competition found itself scrambling to make its own version of the App Store, create software tools, and get programmers on-board to begin making applications for their devices. Companies as varied as Amazon, Microsoft, Nokia, Motorola, and RIM rushed to adapt, also adding touch-screen-based devices to their product lineups.

The combination of smart handheld devices, mobility-enhanced applications, GPS software, and robust wireless Internet experience added up to the promise of mobility. Apple had successfully demonstrated that those companies that effectively execute mobile strategies for commerce, entertainment, and finance would be the winners in the mobile Internet arena. When the movers and shakers behind m-commerce's false start of early 2000s saw the changing tech headwinds, they rejuvenated themselves to bring users banks, shopping malls, entertainment centers, and all of their friends to their palm, pocket, or purse. In early 2010s, nearly 1 billion GPS-enabled phones were starting to transform the entire mobile ecosystem. A new breed of apps was powering payments, location, and mobile ads.

The initial hyperbole unmistakably related to mobile commerce. In the evolution of modern shopping, consumers had very recently progressed from visiting a physical store every time they wanted to buy something to shopping online via a desktop or laptop computer, at least some of the time. The next evolutionary step would presumably have shoppers making more purchases online from mobile devices. Over the years, the smartphone intelligence had been steadily growing in parallel to the device's emerging status of being an important showcase of rich content with handset screens getting bigger and brighter. The sense of shifting sands was further reinforced when 2009 data proclaimed more smartphones being sold than laptop computers.

## M-COMMERCE: A BRIEF HISTORY

Less than a decade after the term "wired" surfed into the public consciousness, heralded a brave new world of wireless Internet that promised to bring forth unprecedented communications power to businesses and ordinary people alike. At the dawn of the new century, when cell phones were singing the happy tones of the Internet, wireless operators saw writing on the wall and began tailoring a variety of new services according to user demands. They promised users would now be able check their bank balances, get weather updates and traffic reports, and read news headlines through innovative new data services. Wireless Internet, as it turned out, was just an icing on the cake; it greatly helped stimulate new industries.

Take mobile e-commerce, or simply m-commerce, which harnessed the ability to make commercial transactions from a cell phone. Back in 1999, in the heady days of dotcom euphoria, it all looked so easy: to make money from the mobile Internet, simply create a mobile version of what worked so well on the fixed-line Internet. The notion of m-commerce quickly became the face of the mobile Internet in a way that was reminiscent to the rise of e-commerce soon after the wired Internet took shape in the commercial arena during the mid-1990s. Then, people would call e-commerce the second chapter of the Internet. Mobile commerce went one step further by promising the ability to purchase goods anywhere through a wireless Internet-enabled device.

The vogue at the time was for business-to-consumer e-commerce, and m-commerce drew a lot of strength from this thriving premise because of the ubiquity of mobile phones. Surely, anything that could be sold over the conventional Internet to PC users could be sold over cellular networks to mobile subscribers. And because mobile users have their phone with them at all times, they might be expected to do more shopping than stationary customers. With the rapidly maturing concept of the mobile Internet, the early backers reasoned, m-commerce could serve as a powerful platform to host new services in collaboration with Amazons and Yahoo!s of the Internet world.

Then there came an interesting twist in the formation of m-commerce prodigy. Although the Internet euphoria spread across the whole globe, when it came to business realties, it was pretty much an American phenomenon. From the super-ISP America Online to the Internet hardware king Cisco to the UNIX server powerhouse Sun Microsystems, almost every predominant company on the Internet scene was of American origin. Hence, when commercial Internet extended its reach to the big-time e-commerce bonanza, it seemed like just another American show. In the ongoing wireless revolution, however, Europe and, to some extent, Asia called the shots. In countries like Japan, where the personal computer penetration was low due to cultural reasons, mobile phones could well become a potent tool to access the plethora of nifty consumer services.

Inevitably, the companies in these parts of the world thought up of m-commerce as an answer to America's e-commerce hegemony. But although European and Japanese footprints were initially predominant in the m-commerce roadmap through projects like WAP and i-mode, when it came to actually doing the Internet, America seemed to know the way forward. It became evident that the Internet-savvy America had still an important role to play in this nascent marketplace when Amazon.com Inc. launched its m-commerce efforts in late 1999. The Seattle–based e-commerce upstart had invented one-click ordering on the Internet that let the buyers store credit card number and address after the purchase. Next up, the online retail pioneer, through its "Amazon Anywhere" initiative, started assembling partnerships with a number of cell phone operators in the United States.

The arrangements typically called for Amazon's website to be given a prominent placement on the screens of mobile phones, critical in those early days because of difficulty users had in navigating the web by punching on a phone keypad. In March 2000, just before the dotcom bubble burst, Amazon chief Jeff Bezos predicted that by 2010, all of his firm's customers would use wireless devices to make purchases. Describing m-commerce as "the most fantastic thing that a time-starved world has ever seen," he predicted that it would change the way people shop, since they would be able to make impulse purchases anywhere, at anytime. Within five to ten years, he claimed, "almost all of e-commerce will be on wireless gadgets." In an industry not yet humbled by the dotcom collapse, Bezos wasn't alone in seeing the wireless web-based mobile commerce as the next big sensation.

Market analysts queued up to make rosy forecasts of m-commerce revenues. With such a bonanza conceivably around the corner, it's no wonder that wireless operators paid so much for the 3G licenses. But when the Nasdaq crashed and the dotcoms started going under, the wireless world came to a rude awakening that making money was hard enough even on the conventional Internet, where technology was rather mature. Once-fashionable dotcoms had failed to bring a workable business model and were now burning in style. The dotcom fiasco had shown to the world the ugly side of the Internet. Now the prospect of buying things on cell phones, with their tiny screens and keypads, suddenly looked far-fetched. The surveys conducted after the dotcom crash showed that consumers found the reality of m-commerce hugely disappointing.

In the hindsight, the way America Online, Yahoo!, and Amazon approached the wireless Internet was to take what they had on the wired web and simply put that on the handset. Another problem with the mobile Internet was that there were too many clicks. An early trial found that it took over forty minutes to order a book by cell phone. Likewise, booking a hotel room on a mobile hotel-reservation system required thirty-seven clicks. Then there were those dreaded lessons from the e-commerce chapter. For instance, its ad-based revenue model had initially proved untenable, leaving many in the wireless industry wondering whether consumers would be the ones to pay for mobile services. Banner ads, pop-ups and the like were deemed failures in the wireless domain. On the heels of this confusing picture, online merchants started placing a low priority on developing and marketing m-commerce services. The user base also remained small because only a few mobile websites were equipped to accept m-commerce transactions.

## THE ENGINE OF M-COMMERCE

So what was the reality of m-commerce: online shopping done on the run? Was it just another reflection of PC-based Internet commerce or the next Internet joke? In a way, m-commerce was just any wireless data activity that made money for a company along the value chain. So when a mobile-phone user made a restaurant reservation, the amount that the user later paid using cash or credit card could be counted as m-commerce revenue. Under this view, m-commerce, in collaboration with the mobile Internet drive, could potentially bring a myriad of new activities for the wireless industry. For a common user, it was all matter of value. Once the wireless industry worked out this piece of puzzle, m-commerce and other wireless data services could come of age much faster than anticipated.

How the promise of m-commerce would descend successfully to the cyberspace was still a question mark in the early 2000s. But as wireless devices got faster, smarter and cheaper, the hope floated that more effective software platform to power the m-commerce products would subsequently emerge. The broad consensus was that it wouldn't be before 2005 that the world sees the three A's of m-commerce—anything, anytime, anywhere. In the meantime, m-commerce architects had to find ways to complement the desktop web but avoid replicating it. There was little point in making an impulse purchase of a book or a CD if it would then have to be delivered by post. Rather than spend ages pecking at a phone keypad, why not wait until one get home and order in comfort from a PC.

The mobile Internet was different from its fixed-line counterpart in three important aspects. First, a mobile phone was a far more personal device than was a PC. It was likely to be used by only one person, who would probably have the phone with him or her for most of his or her waking hours. Second, in the pre-iPhone era, mobile phone operators could broadly determine what menus and services appeared on their handset screens. The ability to set the default portal was a big advantage for operators because it allowed them to act as gatekeepers. Last, and most important, people knew that using mobile phones cost money, and there was a mechanism for the network operator to charge them for that use. Sending an e-mail over the Internet from a PC was essentially free; sending a text message from a cell phone cost about 10 cents. So users were more likely to pay a mobile premium to do things while on the move.

Beyond the stark contrasts of wired and wireless Internets, another significant challenge for the wireless industry was to make m-commerce a seamless social experience. The traditional Internet had existed for many, many years and was only used by a handful of scientists because it was too complicated. Only after people got reasonably easy way to browse the web did the Internet explode and became a driving force in the economy. The same could happen to the mobile Internet and eventually to mobile commerce. The logical conclusion: make it easy.

Then there was this risk that wireless operators might be tempted to set up "walled gardens" of services and contents, hence restricting users to a handful of approved services that would enable operators to capture a much larger chunk of the expected bonanza in data revenues. In the 1990s, online services such as America Online, CompuServe, and Prodigy operated on the walled-garden principle; but as soon as one of them offered unfettered Internet access, the others had no choice but to follow the suit. The walled-garden model could turn out to be just as unsustainable on the mobile Internet because it annoyed users.

In fact, in the early days of the WAP launch, mobile carriers generally limited the number of sites offered to customers by signing exclusive agreements with content providers, or selecting a package of sites from a content aggregator—a third-party portal or a WAP provider. But subscribers didn't want restrictions on whom they could do business with or which sites they could visit. This strategy backfired as majority of users found the m-commerce experience unsatisfying. Mobile phone companies subsequently removed these restrictions. Mobile commerce was initially written off also because the early versions of Internet-enabled phones, the so-called WAP phones, didn't deliver what they promised. When WAP failed to live up to expectations, there was a backlash for m-commerce. In many ways, WAP became the acid test for m-commerce viability.

Mobile Internet access providers, in this case, the wireless operators, generally charged by usage, either for every minute spent online or for every byte downloaded. This meant that they made money on transporting data, so it made sense to offer users the widest choice of content possible to encourage them to run up transport charges. That's how i-mode worked in Japan; the vast majority of NTT DoCoMo's data revenues came from transport, not the sale of content. The Japanese mobile phone operator generally offered a selection of approved services through its own chosen portal, but also gave subscribers the option of going elsewhere. That's what America Online did with its dial-up Internet service; it offered services such as instant messaging, chat rooms, and e-mail, as well as access to the web.

Wireless industry, primarily made up of traditional telecom service providers, faced an important crossroads. The telecommunications model was predominantly based on a closed architecture. A telecom operating company typically owned the network; provided the transport; supplied the services, such as caller ID and calls waiting; and billed the subscriber directly. But was this model applicable to the convergence of mobility and the Internet? Probably not! The ability to control the entire value chain didn't exist in many industries. Now the convergence of voice and data was testing this model because original expectations of the mobile Internet were largely based on the experience mirroring the wired Internet.

In the open architecture of the Internet, service providers bought the raw bandwidth from a backbone carrier such as UUNet, while end users paid for their connection media: dial-up telephone line, DSL, or cable. Once connected, they could subscribe to and pay for any service and complete transaction at their discretion. The consumer accepted this model in which the transmission of data was separate from the provision of service. Overcoming these expectations was proving a challenge for wireless operators.

The industry players were making all the right noises, but because of the complexities of initiating the technology, m-commerce marketplace simply didn't seem ready in the early 2000s. The key m-commerce players had more than a few months of experience to draw on it. Then there were all these whacky ideas like web-enabled ice cream delivery. While it sounded fascinating to have a refrigerator send users an e-mail to let them know they are out of milk and then send a message to Webvan to bring more, in reality, this only came out as one of those "oh-golly" scenarios.

While the Internet strategy had indeed become indispensable for every wireless company, the problem was that the public seemed unenthused. Mobile phone users at large were not sure what the wireless Internet was because the medium itself was still in its embryonic stage. The slew of companies that once emerged hoping to make it easier to translate the riches of the web in the wireless world also missed one important step. No one bothered to ask consumers what they wanted. The wireline Internet had taken off because it offered users instant gratification to get what they wanted, when they wanted it. Next, mobility started giving users the additional space to get answers when and where they wanted them.

Back in early 2000s, for the wireless Internet, while much had converged, much also remained to be converged. Although consultancy firms had predicted massive m-commerce revenue streams, there were big hurdles—standards, security and presentation—before these vast revenues could be tapped. Many of the mobile consumers' concerns, such as security and privacy, and difficulty with navigation, were reminiscent of worries of the early days of e-commerce, and could eventually be overcome. Still, there were broader problems with using handheld devices for shopping. Compared with PCs, which had large color screens, handheld devices of early 2000s were hopeless for browsing. Scrolling through lists was cumbersome, and features and prices were hard to compare. But the difference between these two worlds also presented a window of opportunity. People carried mobile phones with them everywhere, so it was only a matter of time before all necessary components converged onto the mobile phone, making it even more invaluable.

From 1998 to 2000, m-commerce was on a downward cycle, recovering from over-hyped expectations hindered primarily by the technology gap that existed in the infrastructure for this ambitious new venture. From application development to network speeds and from handset functionality to security protocols, they were all being developed and introduced at different rates which contributed further to the disappointment for early adopters. Then there came the first breakthrough from a humble technology nobody was actually looking at. Just when the nascent m-commerce industry was screaming for applications to give it a kick-start, short message service (SMS)—originally built to exchange small text messages across GSM networks—filled the vacuum by providing tangible services to mobile users.

Up till now the mobile Internet—a core building block of the smartphone anatomy—was considered a prime vehicle for the uptake of m-commerce. Beyond the indispensible wireless Internet, however, there were other trump cards in the m-commerce scheme of things. The next chapter encompasses SMS as a primary enabler of m-commerce while chapters 6 and 7 will delve into how location-based services provided the much-needed impetus for m-commerce industry and made business-on-the-go a compelling value proposition.

Mobile commerce, which had long been a dream of technologists and entrepreneurs alike, got its first practical manifestation from a source no one had envisioned through all these years. For a start, mobile phone operators tailored a variety of text-based services according to perceived user demand and accomplished a modest success. Users could check bank balances, weather updates, traffic reports, and news headlines through SMS. A lot more followed as chronicled in the next chapter.

# 2 M-COMMERCE WITHOUT NET

*"I'll txt u in 10mins when I know wh/ restrnt."*

Two hours after earthquake struck Haiti in January 2007, a texting donation campaign, "Text HAITI to 90999," was up and running. After three days, the effort had raised US$5 million for the American Red Cross, and "Text" and "90999" were in the top-ten trending topics on Twitter. Nine months later, more than US$40 million had been donated by people sending as little as US$5 to US$10 from their cell phones. The millions of dollars the Red Cross raised and collected via text messaging demonstrated how the public had turned a corner with m-commerce. The Red Cross, a well-respected organization, gave a clean way for people to contribute using a mobile phone. It was a major validation about the possibilities of text as well as mobile transactions. Another lesson was that simpler m-commerce technology could also be effective.

In 2008, US$300,000 in text donations went to just over one hundred charities, and within two years, mobile giving in the United States reached US$50 million for as many as five hundred organizations. The mobile-giving industry had the potential to change the face of global philanthropy. The Haiti campaign had proven the possibilities of mobile giving—particularly in response to a high-profile crisis. As easy as it was to mail an envelope or visit a website, the operators behind the mobile giving were now betting that the mobile would be even more effective at capturing the short attention spans of potential givers. Mobile giving did have drawbacks though, including US$10 donation limits and the fact that it could take up to ninety days to deliver funds because phone bills must be paid first. On the contrary, online donors didn't have dollar limits, and their donations could be turned around in as little as two days.

Nevertheless, the Haiti earthquake proved a turning point for SMS-centric communications as this incident demonstrated that text messaging was a great medium to connect with the people and the role it could play in innovative campaigns. Text messaging, being the most commonly used data application on mobile phones, had become a major catalyst in the broad realization of wireless data services. Initially, text messaging was overlooked as a key enabler of m-commerce, both as a method to initiate transactions and as a trigger for wireless data use. That was mainly because despite the popularity of text messaging, revenues generated by SMS services remained relatively small. Secondly, m-commerce without the Internet sounded like an absurdity to many retailers.

But after the Haiti earthquake in 2007, SMS became a business reality and a giant leap for m-commerce viability. Text messaging offered something that m-commerce sites, mobile apps, and even e-commerce sites and e-mail couldn't offer: access to consumers without the Internet connection. Text messages traveled over the same wireless networks as mobile phone calls, and required no Internet access. So when it came to getting as close as possible to customers, tiny text messages hit the bull's-eye.

The very first text message was sent on December 3, 1992 by software programmer Neil Papworth at Vodafone. He sent this message from his computer to the cell phone of Vodafone director Richard Jarvis to wish him "Merry Christmas." It's worthwhile to note that Papworth was working on solving a business problem—how to develop an internal paging system for employees at Vodafone. The first person-to-person text message from handset to handset was sent in Finland next year. At that time, few companies used the text-messaging platform to fulfill the business potential. In fact, text messaging took off in the hands of tech-savvy teens for whom SMS was face saving as well as money saving. Over the years, however, mobile users realized that SMS could be a powerful means of communication for businesses and that it could be used effectively as a tool for internal communications among staff, between employees, and business partners.

The use of the mobile technology as a payment gateway had started in Helsinki in 1997 when a company owned by Coca-Cola installed two mobile-optimized vending machines. These machines accepted payment via text messages. Same year, Merita Bank of Finland launched the first handset-based banking service using SMS. In 1999, the Philippines launched the first commercial mobile payments systems on the platforms provided by the country's two large mobile operators: Globe and Smart. Over the course of years, the idea spread and m-commerce manifestations ranging from mobile banking to mobile credit cards to mobile payments became widespread in Asia and Africa, and in selected European markets.

Other SMS-centric data services enabled by handsets included mobile music, downloadable logos and pictures, gaming, gambling, and advertising. In 1998, the first sale of digital content as a download to mobile phones was made possible when the first downloadable commercial ringtones were released by the Finnish wireless operator Radiolinja. The first mobile news service, delivered via SMS, was also launched in Finland later in 2000. Mobile news services expanded in the coming years with many organizations providing "on-demand" news services through text messages.

The evolving business model made use of the premium-rate text messages as a means of charging for one-off lumps of contribution or content such as ringtones, logos, or horoscope. Users sent a text message to a special number, had the content delivered in the form of a text-message reply, and were charged accordingly. This made SMS a communication channel that consumer companies couldn't ignore. The text-based commerce-like services spread rapidly in early 2000s when countries like Austria and Norway launched mobile parking payments. In Vienna, a majority of people paid car parking fees using their mobile phones. Ten minutes before a user's allotted time was about to expire, he or she got a text alert and the option to extend parking minutes. Austria also offered train ticketing service via mobile device.

Then, in 2002, Dunkin' Donuts pioneered a form of targeted marketing in Rome, Italy through text messages. People were invited to text a shortcode number, and in exchange, they received an SMS voucher for a free donut. In addition, if customers presented the coupon at Dunkin' Donuts, they were entered into a lucky draw for a Piaggio scooter. Later, in spring 2008, Amazon.com accomplished a pioneering milestone in text message retailing when it introduced TextBuyIt service. QVC Inc. followed in the fall that year with the QVC Text Ordering feature.

## SMS CALL TO ACTION

Wireless messaging wasn't non-existent in the United States; it's just that Americans were using their pagers to send and receive messages till early 2000s. Next up, people in the United States got hooked to Internet-based instant messaging services like Yahoo! Messenger. In many ways, SMS was like instant messaging, except that users didn't necessarily have to be in front of a computer or load a particular messenger service. Meanwhile, SMS continued to evolve into a more interactive form and spawned a new generation of instant messaging services on its own. Although regular text messages were limited to 160 characters, costing an average of 10 cents each to send, text messaging could be used to do more than just send a quasi-telegram to other people.

The United States lagged behind Asia and Europe in adopting the texting habit, but once GSM-based American wireless operators noticed a leveling off in their customers' use of talk minutes, they introduced texting options and spent more on marketing them. In 2003, AT&T signed on to sponsor *American Idol*, a television show that had viewers voted by texting to the designated numbers. *American Idol* put texting on the U.S. map and unleashed a new wave of text interaction with television. One of the crucial factors in the successful union of television and text messaging was the availability of special four-, five-, or six-digit numbers called shortcodes. While reality TV shows like *American Idol* allowed viewers to cast votes through text messages, there was more to TV-texting assortment than mere voting. News and current affair shows encouraged viewers to send in comments; game shows allowed viewers to compete; music shows took requests by text message; and broadcasters operated the on-screen chat rooms.

The introduction of prepaid mobile tariffs in which people could pay for their airtime in advance and thereby control their mobile phone expenditure was also the catalyst that accelerated the renewed take-up of SMS. When hundreds of millions of text messages were zapped from handset to handset each day during the early 2000s, the service made about 10 percent of operators' overall revenue. Now the advent of premium text was proving very lucrative as mobile operators charged special rates for messages to particular numbers. The TV-related text messaging now accounted for an appreciable share of wireless operators' data revenues. Operators usually took 40 to 50 percent of the revenue from each message, with the rest divided among the broadcaster, the program maker, and the company providing the message-processing system. Text message revenues now became a vital element of the business model for many television shows.

Short message service was one of the simplest and most useful means of communications and the secret of its success laid in the business model. Now that one of the fastest-growing uses of text messaging was interaction with television, the success of TV-related texting became a stark reminder of how easily an elaborate technology could be unexpectedly overtaken by a simpler, lower-tech approach. The ubiquity of SMS on mobile phones was transformational and the testament of the fact that textophiles in the United States were starting to see voice mail as a waste of time. Text messaging also provided impetus to other wireless initiatives like m-commerce and imaging, just like what the Internet had done for a myriad of wired and wireless communication services.

Another ringing endorsement of the SMS power was Twitter, a micro-blogging digital media channel that let people share 140-character or less text messages over the Internet. Instead of calling each other and distracting people during a specific session or having to text seven different people, individuals could stay in contact over Twitter. In a way, websites like Twitter with postings of no more than 140 characters were creating and reinforcing the habit of communicating in micro-bursts pioneered by SMS. And just like SMS, these sites were pumping out sheer volume. In the early going, many Twitter and Facebook devotees even created settings to alert them, via text message, every time a tweet or message was earmarked for them.

Twitter became a signature social platform and disruptive force in communications, media, culture, politics, and commerce arenas. It took on a life of its own just when SMS had picked up strength in the United States. At that time, for many Americans, typing something on a mobile phone meant messing with T9 text input. So Twitter emerged as an incarnation of the popular text messaging and became known as "the SMS of the Internet." The original codename of the company "twttr" was inspired by Flickr and the fact that American SMS shortcodes were five characters.

Text messaging now became so pervasive in the United States that mobile subscribers sent and received more text messages in a month than they did phone calls: as per data gathered in second quarter of 2008, an average of 357 messages per month compared with 204 phone calls. However, the most compelling use of SMS-based business services was seen in emerging markets like India and Kenya, where a growing number of consumers were using even the most basic cell phones to order food and flowers, do their banking, pay bills, make charitable donations, and buy airline, bus, rail, or movie tickets. In India, Hindus even made advance bookings at temples via mobile phone to reserve the offering of prayers during busy holiday periods.

Nokia, which had largely missed the smartphone movement but was still king of the hill in basic phones, saw an opportunity. The European wireless titan now started gearing the text-based applications toward countries like India that had a plethora of lower-cost phones and a preference for exchanging information through text messages instead of the mobile web. Short message service was low-cost, easy-to-use and didn't require a phone with service plan, and thus helped build services with a very low barrier to adoption. According to a *Forbes* report filed by Elizabeth Woyke, in November 2009, Nokia introduced a set of mobile programs called "Life Tools" that provided agricultural information and educational material to people in rural areas. Later, in October 2010, the Finnish handset giant introduced two mobile applications that let Nokia phone users create chat groups and buy and sell products using text messages.

Unlike Life Tools, which supplied farmers with prices and other information, these applications targeted urban users and encouraged people to communicate with each other, not just consume content pushed to their phones. Take the example of We Meet service, a social-networking application that could be used by families, groups of friends, or small businesses. Users could create chat groups from their contact lists and communicate by sending text messages. The application threaded the messages in chronological order, making it easy to follow the conversation. The effect was something like an instant messaging conversation, but at the fraction of the cost and on devices with no data plans. The service allowed the phone's contact list to add notes about clients and accounts, and linked them tightly to the device's calendar. That way, a merchant could make a note about a future payment in the contact list and have it automatically saved to the phone's calendar as a reminder.

These SMS-based services were designed to be location-aware. But instead of pricey GPS technology, typically found only in high-end phones, it tracked people's location via cellular towers. When people moved, the location updated. It wasn't exactly a digital map, but it served the same function. Another service, called MoMart for "mobile mart," comprised product listings delivered by text message. Interested buyers would subscribe to the service and specify the goods they wanted; the program would then push matches directly to their phones. Listings could be text-only or could include an image embedded into the message. They could also be targeted to particular areas using cell-tower location technology, enabling buyers and sellers to meet in person. Nokia managers liked to compare this digital marketplace to a Craigslist or eBay for India.

These services might not look flashy, but they were still smart. Moreover, these services were customer-driven, not just technology-driven. These simple but innovative services also craftily integrated two of the most promising mobile phone applications: text messaging and location. Clearly, the potential for SMS growth hadn't reached its apex yet. Marketers could go to the next step by making their SMS campaigns relevant and local to see a greater response and return-on-investment.

## M-COMMERCE IN AFRICA

In 2006, cellular industry experts in Kenya, Uganda, and Congo noticed that mobile phone users were using minutes as currency, buying them at one place and texting them somewhere else to be redeemed, with the local mobile agent taking a cut. Till then, the predominant way of money transfer in Kenya was to use bus drivers to send money back from the cities to rural regions. But this was slow and error prone.

Eventually, Vodafone, which owned Safaricom, Kenya's largest mobile carrier, formalized a process which allowed Kenya's rural migrants to send their earnings from Nairobi to back home in the countryside. M-Pesa service, launched in Kenya in 2007, allowed people to send and receive cash through mobile phones, thus replacing banks in ordinary people's lives.

M-Pesa quickly became the poster child for mobile payment services in Africa. Safaricom allowed mobile phone users to pay hard cash to a physical agent in return for a code. The code could then be given to one of Safaricom agents anywhere else in Kenya, and redeemed again for cash. Safaricom had provided a real solution to a real problem. Much of the continent's population lived in rural areas with very little access to banking infrastructure. Now add into the mix an urban workforce sending cash to dependents living in rural areas. Inevitably, with both sender and receiver owning or having access to a mobile phone, M-Pesa was going to be the key to extending banking services to the unbanked. What started at wireless operator Safaricom as a way to pay and collect micro-financing had eventually morphed into a "send money home" service.

M-Pesa, a peer-to-peer mobile payments system that worked without banks or financial services institutes like MasterCard, was administered through IBM for Vodafone, one of the largest wireless operators in the world. By 2011, Safaricom had developed a network of 30,000 stores through which its customers could cash in and out of their M-Pesa mobile wallet accounts. That was 200 times the number of branches operated by the largest bank in Kenya. M-Pesa expanded to include airtime top-up, bill payments, salary payments, M-Kesho banking services, and international money transfer in partnership with Western Union. Businesses in Kenya started accepting M-Pesa as a way to pay bills; in addition to the M-Pesa agents, as of 2011, more than 400 companies and government agencies were using M-Pesa to pay bills and salaries. Some Kenyans even used the M-Pesa service as an informal savings account.

M-Pesa became a case study on how technology could be used to fulfill a need, in this case, easy transactions, as opposed to artificially disrupting an entrenched market that would otherwise be slow to change. The service became so popular that, by 2011, a quarter of Kenyan GDP passed through it. Also, by 2011, four years after launch, a little more than one in three Kenyans had registered an M-Pesa account. M-Pesa also inspired other notable innovations, like Google's May 2012 launch of Beba, a pre-paid card for commuters using Nairobi's local buses. It was most likely a test run for a much larger cashless-payment system. M-Pesa-like systems had also been deployed in places such as Bangladesh, Uganda, Nigeria and the Philippines.

M-Pesa had emerged as a standard for mobile money in developing markets. In early 2013, BBM Money in Indonesia became another prominent case study for messaging-centric commerce when it brought real-time mobile payments to BlackBerry's platform-specific social network and messaging service. The service—launched in collaboration with PermataBank and Monitise Group—allowed BlackBerry users to create a mobile money account attached to their BBM identity, and use that to transfer money to other BBM contacts, as well as purchase airtime credit for their device, or move money to bank accounts.

It would allow millions of Indonesian BBM users to conduct business transactions right in the service where many of them already communicated on business matters, and would allow merchants and others to accept payments with the devices they already owned without requiring the involvement of any third-party device or software. BlackBerry users were not charged for sending money between BBM contacts. BlackBerry was the number one selling smartphone in Indonesia, the fourth most populous country in the world with 240 million people, and BlackBerry Messenger was the dominant short message communication platform in the country. A prominent highlight of the service was that the real-time chat was evolving into real-time engagement by effectively taking a social network and turning it into a payment network.

Short message service was a great communication tool because it commanded an effective integration. For the wireless industry in search for the next big thing, text messaging was probably the closest thing to a killer application. Short message service not only brought a social revolution through a very natural form of interaction, it also offered new ways to use text messaging as a marketing tool. For instance, real-estate agents could send buyers real-time, on-site images from the property, along with text on the brief profile of the place. Then there was text advertizing that allowed companies to do brand building through SMS. All these diverse commercial leanings combined with the proliferation of text messaging could spur growth in the m-commerce arena.

Short message service had been a trusted old friend of mobile marketing mostly because of lower cost, simplicity and the fact that it had been around longer than other mobile marketing techniques. Given that text messages had a broad reach, for well-executed campaigns, the results could be impressive. The primary benefits of SMS were the immediacy, the nearly ubiquitous reach, and almost 100-percent open rate. But SMS also had a problem of image because it was closely associated with feature phones and, therefore, was bypassed when brands started thinking about smartphones. Short message service appeared to have been forgotten when the smartphone burst on the IT scene in late 2000s because marketers got so excited about the richer experiences they could deliver via apps and the mobile web.

Interestingly, despite this unprecedented excitement around the smartphone revolution and the notion that SMS was not needed on smartphones, text messaging was still the most used app on smartphones. The power of smartphones aside, a significant number of mobile users still preferred receiving offers via SMS. An abundance of mobile ads flooding the market didn't discourage a majority of mobile users from being receptive to a good deal served up via SMS. On the merchant side, because text messages had a near 100 percent open rate—compared to e-mails at 74 percent—SMS tended to be an attractive option for businesses. Retailers acknowledged SMS as a critical part of their marketing strategy.

However, SMS was a tricky game. Technically, it was inbound. If overused, SMS carried the risk of irritating customers that were once eager to receive offers, given that a mobile device was perhaps the most personal of all hardware. Moreover,

SMS had significant security vulnerabilities and congestion problems, even though it was widely available and accessible. There was also a host of SMS marketing regulations; for instance, marketing messages to children under thirteen were prohibited.

Another crucial challenge was shortcodes used in SMS campaigns. There were serious hurdles for businesses wanting to leverage SMS marketing in understanding and dealing with the shortcode process. Brands came across serious difficulties in getting shortcodes while working with mobile carriers as they waded through the confusion, ambiguity, and complication of shortcode setup, provisioning, regulation, and best practices. So, for making SMS a viable marketing channel, shortcodes had to be made more affordable and the processes had to be simplified. Another key step in lowering the barrier of entry for acquiring and using shortcodes related to addressing the regulatory scrutiny for large and small businesses alike.

So, after the launch of the iPhone, mobile commerce thrust gradually moved away from SMS platforms and into actual commerce-centric applications. The next chapter will cater to m-commerce 2.0 that was reinvigorated through the marvel of the iPhone and apps it brought to life.

# 3 HERE COMES THE iPHONE

*"Every once in a while a revolutionary product comes along that changes everything. It's very fortunate if you can work on just one of these in your career. … Apple has been very fortunate in that it has introduced a few of these."*

— Steve Jobs, the Apple co-founder and former CEO, announcing the iPhone in January 2007

The mobile Internet's troubled youth was a form of natural progression in the evolution of m-commerce. Mobile commerce generated a huge buzz when introduced during the late 1990s, but with the exception of NTT DoCoMo's i-mode offering, it had been a major disappointment. Due to network and handset shortcomings and limited content available on WAP and other data services, potential customers were not enthused and failed to sign on in large numbers. Mobile commerce went through a lot in its brief existence and the insight this learning curve garnered from failures of wireless operators, content providers, and WAP service companies proved to be immensely valuable. For instance, wireless industry began to ponder on why had m-commerce been a hit in Japan only?

One of the primary reasons of WAP failure was that services were launched before they were ready. Moreover, mobile phone networks were inadequate for handling the commerce-like shopping experience that was promised to subscribers. Mobile commerce was a bright idea whose time could come once the wireless industry came over its apathy for embracing data services. However, the basic problem with mobile data in general, and m-commerce in particular, was that there was no clear business model. The remedy would require the transformation of the existing telecom practices into entirely new business models and it was an uphill task. But if done well, mobile phones, for instance, could emerge as a popular vehicle of payment, at least for small items. Since wireless operators were used to handling large numbers of small transactions, their billing systems could manage such transactions at around a tenth of the cost of a bank or a credit card company.

Unlike on the fixed-line Internet, people were prepared to pay for content and services they really wanted. But they preferred to pay lumpy subscription fees rather than a small charge for every morsel of information they accessed. Once past the initial stumbling blocks, mobile commerce, being rife with opportunities, could kick-start in several fast-growing niches: for example, provision of services to stock traders and others who need instant information. Mobile commerce could also transform stores into virtual showrooms. Handsets with bar-code scanners would let users purchase and customize a product and have it waiting for them when they get home. A person looking for a new apartment or a house, while driving in a particular neighborhood, saw a "for rent" or "for sale" sign with a code listed on the signboard. He or she could key in the code into cell phone to receive short video clips of the interior and decide about arranging a visit.

In many ways, the mobile Internet in 2005 was at the same stage of development as its wired counterpart was in 1995 when the web was in its infancy. Then, retailers asked if the e-commerce channel was for real. Could it be used as a competitive channel? There were hundreds of startups, and nobody really knew which technologies and business models would win, or what consumers or corporate users wanted. But this cycle of boom and gloom on e-commerce trail also meant that there were plenty of lessons to be learned from the mis-takes made on the fixed-line Internet. While which model would prove most successful remained to be seen, there was certainly money sloshing around on the mobile Internet.

By late 2000s, most of the pieces of the puzzle that had to be in place to make m-commerce successful were already in place. Text messaging had provided m-commerce with initial traction and necessary learning curve, but SMS had mostly been successful as an appetizer. That's probably because text messaging was primarily a marketing vehicle; when it came to making purchases, the action was on mobile websites. Only fully transactional m-commerce sites would enable consum-ers to shop more or less as they would on an e-commerce site, except on a pared-down version. It was also imperative that m-commerce sites provide shoppers access to the same number of products as e-commerce sites.

The search for the "killer application" went on until the iconic iPhone came, bringing a revolution in the way people look and use their mobile phones. The iPhone was the first mass market mobile device that made the Internet fun and easy to use, especially on websites optimized for mobile phones. Once phones and the mobile Internet converged on powerful new platforms, like the iPhone, more consumers started using the mobile web as a viable communication tool. Devices like the iPhone boasted significant computing power and made accessing the Internet from a handset far easier than with mainstream feature phones.

Retailers had heard the m-commerce mantra before. A lot of retailers that had earlier invested resources and effort in the mobile market were disappointed in results, which generally stemmed from consumers' poor experiences on conventional mobile phones. Also, in the early stages, mobile-optimized sites were quite dumbed-down; they were basic versions of websites that reminded users of clunky web pages of the early 1990s. And the fully capable mobile Internet devices were not there yet. The iPhone changed all that. The game-changing smartphone set the bar for a true mobile browsing experience in which sites rendered the way they would on a PC. Consumer expectations went up: they had good experiences with some mobile sites, and now they were expecting standard websites of other companies to offer a good mobile experience as well.

The slick new phones with great visual experiences and added functionality like GPS location awareness changed everything. Just as broadband Internet made shopping online far more attractive, so too, did these powerful smartphones by changing the game of m-commerce. Now retailers were lining up to learn the rules of the m-game. The post-iPhone era saw a flurry of retailers creating text messaging-based marketing programs, m-commerce sites and downloadable mobile applications to reach out to consumers who wanted to do more with their phones. eBay, for example, reported a whopping US$380 million in sales through its iPhone app and m-commerce site for the first nine months of 2009. A Nordstrom app replaced a salesperson with a whole new in-store experience.

Wireless companies initially touted m-commerce as a mobile extension of e-commerce instead of portraying it as a unique, value-added mobile service. So they found users flocking to the wired web and ignoring the mobile alternative. Customizing m-commerce to multiple consumer tastes, as shown by DoCoMo's i-mode service, launched nearly eight years before the arrival of iPhone, offered better chance of success. The i-mode service allowed Japanese mobile users to utilize their phones for most of their everyday transactions. They could purchase a plane ticket and use the e-statement stored on the phone to check into the flight. They could locate nearby convenience stores or vending machines using mobile GPS and then make the purchase from the device itself.

Like its remarkable mobile Internet execution, Apple seemed to have learned all the right lessons from the success of i-mode in the m-commerce realm. Like DoCoMo, Apple carefully cultivated an entire ecosystem made up of thousands of apps, which in turn, made it possible for people to go beyond the mobile web to get things done. The company that had put MP3 players in the hands of the masses and had changed the way consumers interacted with music was now courting software developers to build a brand new industry around its iPhone platform. By 2010, the iPhone was at the center of a huge m-commerce maelstrom with thousands of alluring apps. An increasing number of consumers armed with smartphones like the iPhone were relying on online product reviews and recommendations while in the aisles of brick-and-mortar retail outlets.

## FOURTH SALES CHANNEL

Now retailers were nervously looking at the m-commerce bandwagon on its way to joining stores, catalogs and websites as a mainstream retailing channel. Mobile commerce was on way to becoming the fourth sales channel. In the hindsight, wireless Internet and its alter ego m-commerce were not a wishful thinking at all. It's just that wireless industry in general and retailers in specific needed to think through their mobile strategy from the ground-up. The m-commerce affair was a lot like e-mail; in the early 1990s, e-mail wasn't hot but later became the killer app of the Internet and caused the demise of fax. Almost everything could be communicated via e-mail. Just like e-mail, the infrastructure for m-commerce needed to be in place, and once it was there, people wouldn't think twice about joining the m-commerce foray.

In retrospect, the 2001 version of Amazon's m-commerce site was bare bones compared with 2009's Amazon Anywhere, which according to the company reports, was able to yield significant traffic gains. Over the years, the e-retailer added features and functions based on customer e-mails and comments that came in through the Feedback buttons. By 2010, Amazon was selling over US$1 billion annually via mobile devices. What the world's largest e-retailer had learned through a decade of experience was that how it sold on the wired web couldn't be ported straight to the mobile world. That crucial inflection point hidden in the twilight zone of wired and wireless Internets for many years was finally becoming evident to the industry by 2010.

But mobile commerce was still in its infancy in 2010 because mobile Internet-enabled phone users were more likely to employ their devices to get weather forecasts, read news, find movie times, and bank online than buy products. The i-mode case study suggested that users may be prepared to pay a small amount to receive news, weather, sports scores, horoscope, and so on. But though subscription revenues associated with these services were tiny, the real money could be in transport. Mobile operators would most likely make money on m-commerce and location-based services, if only through the associated transport revenues. Access to free content, such as train timetables, would also enhance transport revenues. However, there was a group in the wireless industry who believed that the real value proposition for wireless operators might not be in the ability to own spectrum and provide the transport, but in their ability to differentiate by offering unique services that end users would find valuable or entertaining.

But there came the rub: wireless operators were still largely focused on voice, which accounted for the bulk of their revenue. Voice could remain the epicenter of wireless communications for the foreseeable future because everyone needs to speak. At the same time, however, moving forward to the new data paradigm, new forms of communications would inevitably evolve. The innovative new services built around location, m-commerce and personalization could harness a new business foundation for mobile phone companies. People were starting to use their mobile phones to send and receive data in increasingly interactive manners. Although mobile sales could be slow initially, a big bubble could eventually come through the air pipe and deliver a major wake-up call, showing everyone just how important this sales channel was. With mobile Internet usage expected to surpass desktop, at some point in the future nearly all media consumption could be untethered.

Wireless industry had first started pondering m-commerce for transaction-based services, but then messaging services came up first with rich content to follow. There were image, video and media streaming technologies that promised a new world of multimedia possibilities. Sharper color screens on mobile phones made wireless data services more appealing. The collection of these features and services would get to the core of what m-commerce and wireless Internet had been promising all along. The combination of personalization, location, and willingness to pay made all kinds of business models possible. That could turn m-commerce into a powerful new engine for smartphone take-up while entertainment was likely to become the significant secondary source of smartphone revenues.

## MOBILE COMMERCE 2.0

It wasn't until 2008 that m-commerce really began to grow, helped in large part by the advent of the iPhone, which generated enormous excitement for m-commerce despite holding only a small chunk of the global smartphone market. Apps largely moved m-commerce off the web and onto a more secure mobile Internet platform. They cut through the clutter of domain-name servers and uncalibrated information sources, taking users straight to the content they valued.

Before the iPhone came along, businesses had one simple question: "What should we be doing on mobile?" In the post-iPhone era they were unanimous in their agenda: "We should be doing an iPhone app." With apps, the smartphone suddenly became the epicenter of the software world. With an app phone in a user's hand, which was like a mini computer, a revolution was knocking at the door and it was like the PC saga all over again. Take the case of gaming, which exploded on the iPhone platform in 2009, especially with fantastic shooters such as *Alive-4ever;* with quality game-play and graphics it looked like something seen on an Xbox 360. Then there were apps like UberCab, which allowed consumers to call a taxi. These early apps either served as a utility tool or provided some kind of entertainment. But as it turned out, there were bigger opportunities hidden in the apps domain.

The next year, in 2010, smartphones started to change the e-commerce equation by enabling shoppers to bring the means of buying online straight into a traditional store. Amazon's Price Check—a free iPhone app—let users check prices of CDs, DVDs, books, and video games on the fly by scanning products, snapping a photo, saying the product name, or typing in the name, brand, or model numbers. Price Check burned away the awkwardness of typing the names of individual items into tiny search boxes by building a barcode scanner into the app. The days when consumers merely crawled through newspaper ads and trekked out to brick-and-mortar stores were gradually coming to an end. The power of the smartphone and the tablet had just given them more options than ever.

Amazon was joined by competitors such as eBay, which let users search prices and compare results with its RedLaser barcode scanning mobile app. In 2010, eBay bought this barcode-scanning app from Occipital, a software maker based in Boulder, Colorado, and integrated the technology into its own iPhone and Android apps. Just like Amazon, while pursuing multichannel retailing, eBay wanted to find ways to tap the expanding market for mobile commerce. But unlike Amazon, however, eBay's primary business comprised of connecting third-party sellers with shoppers. Mobile was now a central part of eBay's strategy to insure its brand overhaul from auction site to a "buy anything anywhere with any device" platform. Moreover, as the world's biggest online auction site, eBay aimed for mobile purchases to boost revenue at PayPal—its online-payment unit with 100 million plus active registered accounts and the fastest-growing part of the company.

Smartphone had turned into an ultimate a price-transparency device. While trolling stores, shoppers could compare prices and read reviews on similar products available from Amazon or the company's retail partners. That way the Seattle–based company encouraged smartphone-equipped consumers to link to its payments page and make a transaction. Customers who downloaded the app and enabled the location feature would also merit an additional 5 percent discount of up to $5 on Amazon's products. The service made it very easy for users to order the item via the app: With one phone tap, the often lower Amazon price for the item materialized in front of mobile user. A few more taps, and that item was on the way to mobile user's house. Showrooming became a no-brainer.

The practice of shoppers looking at a product in the store, comparing prices and buying it online became so common that it earned a name—showrooming. Smartphones had raised the showrooming threat to a new level since price comparisons were available to shoppers immediately, as they made decisions and browsed e-commerce websites in stores. Showrooming had brought the e-commerce threat directly to bricks-and-mortar retailers; holiday season sales were particularly impacted by showrooming. A study revealed that JC Penney—which had a disastrous 32 percent decline in same-store sales for the fourth quarter of 2012—was at risk from showrooming because showroomers visited its locations 14 percent more frequently during the holiday season than the average U.S. shopper did in January 2013.

Initially, retailers frowned on shoppers visiting their stores merely to scope out products and buying them online for less. Some retailers took drastic measures to curb the practice, such as blocking barcodes. But while the efforts to stop showrooming were understandable, it was likely futile because the practice would only expand with the proliferation of smartphones. So brick and mortar retailers reluctantly began to acknowledge showrooming as a standard practice.

Recognizing their defeat, in 2012, many retailers made a u-turn and began helping shoppers get online through their smartphones. Big U.S. retailers like Target, J.C. Penney, and Saks Fifth Avenue installed free Wi-Fi throughout their stores. Macy's and Sam's Club had deployed Wi-Fi a year earlier while Nordstrom did so in 2010.

But showrooming wasn't the only thing going on. Smartphones had tunneled their way into nearly every dimension of daily life, a reality some of the biggest forces in retail now seemed to be confronting head-on. Whether online or offline, companies were recognizing that people would use their phones to shop. Some of the biggest names in the retail business were now rolling out their own mobile commerce platforms to lure consumers. A Starbucks app let users load cash onto their mobile phones, which then displayed a barcode that could be scanned at the register. Eventually, Amtrak, Boston's light rail commuter service, Tabbedout, and T.G.I. Fridays started offering mobile payments using the virtual card model following the Starbucks app.

Walmart also recognized the fact that no one left the smartphone in the car before coming in to the store and didn't try to build a fence to block showrooming. In 2011, Amazon's sales were more than five times those of Walmart online, no doubt some of them generated via Amazon Price Check in a Walmart store. So the world's largest retailer pursued the meshing of mobile with offline shopping more aggressively than any other traditional retailer. Walmart launched its own app that had a barcode scanner of its own and let shoppers keep a running total of what was in their physical shopping cart. When shoppers entered the store, the location-aware app switched over to in-store mode automatically and pointed shoppers to discounts, coupons, and what was on sale.

Apple, who had built up a portfolio of 200 million credit card accounts through its iTunes store, had caused enormous disruption at the brick-and-mortar chains. In the hindsight, it might not be a mere coincidence that in 2010 the industry began to see the struggles of conventional stores. During this year, Barnes and Noble put itself up for sale and Blockbuster filed for bankruptcy. Mobile had turned the traditional sales cycle on its head by giving customers the ability to quickly browse and compare prices from competing outlets, effectively turning big box giants like Best Buy into showrooms for online retailers. Moreover, phones and tablets made for a 24/7 digitally-connected world. The pressure to make an in-store purchase evaporated when a consumer knew she could buy from her iPhone or iPad later after further consideration.

The iPhone launch was a defining moment for the nascent m-commerce industry. After the iPhone-driven commerce gathered initial momentum, many in the industry started taking a more rounded, holistic approach that embraced not only payment apps, but also mobile-optimized sites, mobile advertising, mobile coupons and tickets, and location-based services. The next couple of chapters attempt to delve into the payment domain primarily in the context of mobile shopping and see how mobile payments technology fits into the bigger m-commerce picture.

# 4 THE MAKING OF THE MOBILE WALLET

*"This is a big opportunity for the mobile industry. The payment industry is larger than the entire wireless industry."*

— Jaymee Johnson, head of marketing for Isis

Want to swap data wirelessly, pair an accessory, make a payment or check in by just tapping the mobile phone against something else? Near field communication (NFC) technology was what made it happen. The next class act in turning the smartphone into a kind of electronic wallet centered on the NFC platform which allowed data transmission over very short distances. An NFC chip embedded into a phone would allow a user to make a wireless payment just by waving the handset in front of NFC-enabled readers at subway stations, drug stores, and taxicabs. Ironically, reminiscent of the location saga, it was Nokia who first brought this technology to its 5140 handset back in 2004. And, in a classic case of déjà vu, it was Google who stole the early march when it launched an NFC-based mobile wallet in May 2011. The episode was another stark reminder of Nokia's inability to turn expensive research into a product that people really wanted.

While Nokia had made an early bid to bring NFC technology onto mobile phones, the NFC technology was born in the early 2000s through a partnership between Sony and Philips Electronics, and had its roots in the transport and convenience store segments in large Asian cities like Hong Kong. Near field communication was an extension of radio frequency identification (RFID) technology which had been employed in the electronic tags used in toll-road systems. Now, courtesy of NFC magic, 2011 was predicted to be the year of mobile transaction's ascent into mainstream. Mobile commerce advocates said that cash would become a thing of the past and that the future of digital money was in smartphones. A phone was a lot smarter than a card and retailers would welcome the flexibility and rich experience it offered at the point of sale. Smartphones were disruptive because they integrated multiple capabilities into a single device.

Until now, the financial use of smartphones was mostly limited to checking bank balances, buying ringtones, or using a mobile Internet browser to make an online purchase. Mobile wallet referred to the digital replacement for traditional credit cards and debit cards that could be loaded into a phone and used for payment. The information stored on the magnetic strip of a credit or debit card would now reside on the NFC part of the mobile handset, and that would inevitably turn phones into a mobile wallet. The selling point for mobile payments would not be just faster check-out but a plethora of novel apps that developers would build on top of the mobile wallet. Near field communication would serve as glue in a retail payment ecosystem that offered a central repository for bank account information, coupons, loyalty points, and membership cards in just a single tap of a phone.

In the early going, when the industry saw mobile payments through rose-colored glasses, Google launched a pilot project, leveraging MasterCard's PayPass platform and boasting acceptance of 124,000 merchants across the United States. The initiative was launched with just Citibank as a partner, thus limiting the number of consumers who could take full advantage of the system. Although Google barely made a ripple with its mobile wallet offering, all who used the NFC-based mobile wallet on their smartphones to pay for physical goods agreed on one thing: mobile payments were cool. With a swipe of a phone on a point-of-purchase NFC tag, mobile users could buy coffee, cigarettes, and other items.

Google Wallet was the first large-scale effort at transforming the way people paid. Google engineers Rob von Behren and Jonathan Wall conceived the idea of Google Wallet in 2009 using their free "20 percent" time that allowed the company employees to spend one fifth of their work time on projects of their choice. Their idea of mobile wallet remained in wilderness until 2010 when it was rescued by the newly arrived vice-president of commerce, Stephanie Tilenius, an eBay and PayPal veteran. Subsequently, the trio took the project to the Android team where they drew the final blueprint of an

NFC-based mobile wallet. Google then methodically lined up all the pieces it needed to make a big push on the NFC platform for contactless payments. But the playing field was still new and Google was testing the waters.

The digital media behemoth wasn't taking a cut of Google Wallet transactions but coveted the payment data to better target users with deals. Gaining a bigger foothold in the wireless payment market would help solidify Google's role as the leading seller of ads on phones and other mobile devices. The Internet giant was in the business of selling ads across all digital channels, from search to banners to web television; the use of the wallet would be free but with the quid pro quo that Google got to use the purchase data. With a sleek interface and ad-based business model, Google Wallet was a bold step in the right direction. Then there came the first major roadblock to Google's ambitious game plan. Verizon blocked Google Wallet from mobile devices operating on its network. The second largest U.S. wireless operator actually prevented Android handset makers from putting NFC devices onto phones. Sprint was the only U.S. mobile operator that eschewed the carrier-driven mobile payment initiative Isis and got fully behind Google's NFC platform.

Near field communication—a closely watched technology— was also the common thread in the battle for the control of the mobile wallet among four major stakeholders: smartphone makers, apps developers, credit card companies, and wireless operators. Mobile phone players such as Apple, Google, and RIM wanted to put NFC chips directly into handsets and upgrade the respective phone operating systems accordingly. Once payment credentials were directly stored on handsets, third-party app developers and handset makers could jointly create payment solutions, facilitate transactions and redemption of coupons and discounts, and gain insight into consumer spending behavior.

Wireless carriers, on the other hand, wanted the NFC part to be embedded into a phone's SIM card, which in turn, would make it easier to switch to any handset enabled for NFC transactions. It was simply a matter of competing visions, and just like phone makers, wireless operators wanted to get hold of the consumer account data and bind users to their own services. In fall 2010, the three large wireless operators in the United States—AT&T, T-Mobile, and Verizon—chalked out their own battle plan through an m-commerce venture dubbed as Isis. They also partnered with a payment process-ing firm, Discover Financial Services Inc., and a card issuer in Barclaycard to bring relevant expertise into this venture. Eventually, in 2011, Isis was able to lure all major credit card companies—American Express, MasterCard and Visa—into the fold.

Google's efforts to do away with the physical wallet only met a slow adoption and barely made a dent in what was expected to be a giant market opportunity. Google Wallet, which was primarily limited to Sprint, US Cellular and Virgin devices, boasted support at 200,000 locations, but only about twenty national retail chains supported Google Wallet's full experi-ence with offers. Evidently, there were many hurdles facing widespread adoption of mobile payments. Not surprisingly, therefore, Google remained somewhat coy about its wallet ini-tiative while insisting it was working on partnership with the banks and financial institutions rather than trying to supplant them. The Internet media giant was inevitably going to experience pain points on the way to mass adoption with every new partner it brought into its mobile payment ecosystem.

Amid all this uncertainty, by 2013, NFC-based payments were still a rarity despite Google's big marketing push. If NFC payments were only about transferring money from one point to another, this would not be an issue. The promise of mobile payments, however, went so much deeper. Deals, discounts, offers, streamlined digital receipts, location-based coupons, loyalty rewards, and other services that smartphones made possible were the major allure of mobile payments. The mobile wallet could offer promotions that were highly personalized.

## DUMB PIPE SYNDROME

Mobile payment was now the new battlefield in the mobile telecom industry with companies fighting to offer consumers a way to pay for purchases with their smartphones instead of physical wallets. The payment industry was larger than the entire wireless industry. This was a once-in-lifetime opportunity for the mobile phone business so the wireless operators were attempting to draw a line. With Isis, they were trying to create a platform where they would be able to compete not just in payments, but all the marketing goodies that would be associated with them. The mobile phone operators clearly wanted to use their leverage to ensure that they were not locked out of the multi-billion dollar mobile payment push.

Now Google needed to quickly figure out how it was going to gain traction in a business that was attracting all sorts of competitors. The Google Wallet episode and the subsequent response of the U.S. wireless operators also solved the mystery of why NFC wasn't part of the iPhone 4S handset that Apple launched during the same time frame when Google Wallet came to life. Then a notable boost for the Isis project came from an unexpected corner: Microsoft's Windows Phone platform would play the NFC game by the rules set by the wireless operators comprising the Isis camp. Clearly, it was a window of opportunity for the newly launched Windows Phone operating system software to gain leverage in the mobile payment arena against mega competitors: Apple and Google.

Windows Phone 8 would feature a wallet hub where users could store their credit and debit card information, third-party loyalty and membership cards, coupons, and deals. The Windows Phone Wallet experience would also support NFC tap-to-pay, but unlike Google Wallet, the credit and debit card information would be stored in a secure SIM card, not in an on-device system. Moreover, Microsoft incorporated embedded tags that transferred product information directly to Windows Phone with a simple tap of the phone on top of the advertisements.

While Apple wasn't among the early adopters of this burgeoning technology, Google found itself in the re-evaluation phase after three large U.S. operators railroaded its mobile wallet platform. Google, following the slow adoption of its mobile wallet initiative, began considering sharing revenue with wireless operators to get them on-board. Another option was sidestepping mobile phone operators altogether and relying more heavily on in-store terminals to complete mobile payment transactions. This approach could entail additional hardware and software for POS terminals, which would be directly connected to Google's servers inside the cloud. So instead of requiring phones to authenticate payments—something that needed assistance from mobile phone operators—the system might send transactions to Google servers for approval and then clear it with the retailer.

Google, who endured the backlash from mobile phone carriers, first began to reorganize its mobile wallet around its apps platform—now called Google Play—while encouraging developers not to use other payment methods like PayPal and Boku. A platform with hundreds of millions of stored credit cards carried a huge leverage in an m-commerce enterprise. There were only three firms on the planet who had stored over a hundred million active credit card numbers that one could think of: Amazon, Apple, and PayPal. Apple, already riding a frenzy of the iPhone and the iPad popularity, could become a trillion dollar company if it succeeded in pulling off the same success in the m-commerce realm. And it would be interesting to see whether competitors such as Google and Isis had enough of a head start to stave off Apple's push when it would eventually come.

Mobile phone services were a big business but revenue per user had started to flat-line by 2010. Mobile phone users were spending more and more on games and apps that were not sold by wireless operators. Now the biggest fear that the wireless operators had was that they would be turned into dumb pipes without any control of the content and data flowing over their networks. The U.S. mobile operators' empire of controlling content, distribution, and policy suffered the biggest blow in 2007 when the iPhone became the first mainstream device that didn't start up on a carrier-owned phone screen. It was a huge inflection point and symbolized mobile carriers being pushed to become the dumb pipes they had long dreaded. Not surprisingly, therefore, the wireless industry partnerships had started to mature around the globe as a call for action before Google got its foot in the door. Rogers and CIBC joined hands in Canada while Britain's largest carriers were forming their own Isis-like joint venture.

In the United States, the mobile phone operators were adjusting to a new power dynamic in which the "big four" of the new tech establishment—Amazon, Apple, Facebook and Google—were setting the trends and coming over the top to eat their margins and consumer mindshare. Amazon with its US$34 billion online retail operation and Facebook with a 900 million-strong user base could make a play for the mobile payment pie. Apple and Google were already leading the charge with an active culture of innovation. Apple, for instance, enjoyed great relationships with consumers, more pull with physical retailers than PayPal, and stakes in the smartphone market which could provide the firm with leverage to turn NFC into a payment standard. Apple and Google were several years ahead of the wireless operators in product development and wireless operators could see writing on the wall. As a result, reactionary instincts led to a strong push behind m-commerce platforms from archrivals like AT&T and Verizon as they tried to establish a presence and develop a customer base before the "big four" juggernaut rolled into town.

Mobile phone operators didn't have a good track record in technology innovation. But with Isis they were not trying to solve a technology problem but attempting to make mobile payments work on scale. Scale was crucial to get mobile commerce off the ground. Mobile phone operators were experts at processing payments by virtue of phone calls and text messages being processed and charged. They made for a great "retail distribution network" and could effectively serve to educate consumers on mobile payments. So, over time, Isis began to be seen as serious about being a contender. The mobile wallet platform inked deals with POS partners like Verifone, Ingenico and ViVOtech and handset makers such as HTC, LG, Motorola Mobility, RIM, and Samsung. The fact that all of these companies—from credit card firms to banks to startups—were trying to enmesh themselves into the Isis venture made it a 500-pound gorilla in the mobile payment space, at least on paper. Now a more confident Isis went by the slogan "national mobile commerce venture that will fundamentally transform how people shop, pay and save."

Isis shifted gears in spring 2012, when instead of focusing on getting a slice of the payments it opened up the platform to banks and credit card companies and began talking about the opportunity of delivering targeted offers to mobile users. The business model didn't involve a direct cut of the credit-card fees charged to merchants. Instead, issuers were expected to pay to get their cards carried in the wallet, and merchants would pay to extend loyalty rewards and redeem special offers. As a result, the three-carrier consortium was able to bring an armada of partners: all the major credit card brands, three banks with 100 million customers, and makers of merchant terminals and phone handsets.

The banking partners of Isis—including Barclaycard, Capital One and Chase—who gave the venture access to about 50 percent of consumers in the United States, would place their credit, debit and pre-paid cards on the Isis app. The banks could also add their own features inside the Isis app. They could include recent transaction history, the ability to pay bills, or provide social offers or rewards to their card holders. Isis clearly understood the need to provide more value than just an alternative to a card swipe and was looking to go beyond merely a simple payment alternative. On the other hand, banks and financial institutions desperately wanted to be tied into the mobile payments ecosystem.

Isis' wave-and-pay network missed its scheduled launch in summer 2012 but finally went live in hundreds of retail locations throughout Austin and Salt Lake City in October that year. The Isis program required a special SIM card in the handset and an NFC chip. To activate the service, a user must go into the store to get an Isis SIM card and must also download the Isis app. After selecting a personal identification number (PIN) the mobile user had an option of choosing to link a credit card or use a pre-paid option that he or she would top up using a credit card. The transaction process was generally smooth: the mobile user would whip out his phone, open the app, enter his PIN and then tap it against the contactless payment tab. He would click a button that said "OK," and he was done. The Isis service user could link multiple cards to the app and choose which one he wanted to use.

Next, the venture began to conceive Twitter-like feeds inside the Isis app that would allow mobile users to follow stores they liked and get updates from them. When merchants integrated the Isis commerce stack into their payment terminals, they would be able to provide product updates and new offers after a consumer checked out through the Isis app. However, while Isis was not attempting to become a bank or a payment network, some industry watchers still saw its business model as shortsighted and flawed. Isis was seeking to charge banks a fee just to allow a bank's customers to load cards into the Isis mobile wallet. Card issuers owned the customers, and faced with a fee, they could steer customers to use other mobile wallets. Isis, for instance, could have chosen to concentrate on adoption in the near term, not extracting a quick buck from crucial partners. Unsurprisingly, all major credit card companies, while continuing to court Isis, were pushing their own wallet and payment solutions as well.

When it came to payment experience, it seemed more convenient than cash, but less convenient than a credit card—mostly because of all the entering a PIN, swiping and then clicking OK, then manually refreshing to see what the balance was to confirm the amount. Then, not only was Isis unsupported in all but a few handsets, many stores that were supposed to participate in the launch had never heard of the program. The Isis service mostly mirrored that of its major rival, Google Wallet, and now it was facing similar limitations in its trials in Austin and Salt Lake City. Both Isis and Google Wallet relied on NFC technology, which needed to be present in both the handset and point-of-sale terminal. They both had tried to create new payments systems from scratch and had concluded it was far too costly and painful to deal with regulators, set up anti-fraud systems and so forth.

Isis was planning to make its mobile wallet service available all over the United States by the end of 2013.The way Isis steadily kept adding critical pieces to its payment ecosystem impressed many in the industry. Conversely, however, some industry observers saw Isis as moving too slowly in a fast moving sector where the goal was to establish a platform. The consortium of U.S. telecom operators seemed to believe that NFC wouldn't become a mainstream technology overnight, so it was lining up all the necessary components while not committing to an aggressive timeline to ensure that merchants and mobile users didn't sour on their first experiences with Isis. However, while Isis was seen as getting a lukewarm response, the temperature was gradually rising in the mobile payments space. Isis was walking a fine line here and the failure of the venture meant that wireless service providers would continue their slow march toward commoditization.

## APPLE A CONSPICUOUS HOLDOUT

Despite the fact that Google Wallet was seen as having failed the test run and that Isis was perceived as being too cautious and too slow, the NFC-based mobile wallet initiative was still considered the foundation of a new, disruptive payment operating system. The imminent battle over the mobile payments gold was going to be the stuff of legends. Never had so many corporate giants been lined up for their piece of the pie. Ironically, however, there was one company missing in mobile payments action and that company had a track record of busting through roadblocks such as the ones faced by the mobile payments bandwagon. Apple had done it with the combination of iPod and iTunes, with the iPhone, and with the iPad. The Silicon Valley veteran had mastered the art of driving industry participation even in circumstances when the business case for participating was tenuous. Moreover, its iconic iPhone and iPad gadgets had both mindshare and market share to push mobile payment adoption to a tipping point.

There was a widespread perception that NFC wouldn't take off until it was built into the iPhone. Industry watchers had maintained that eventually, when Apple incorporated NFC into the iPhone, it would be the true harbinger of the hey-day for mobile payments. Many in the industry saw Apple as the only company who was capable of catalyzing adoption of tap-to-pay on smartphones. They reckoned that Apple wouldn't take any fee and transaction charges to dodge early barriers to adoption and its real prize would simply be a boost in sales of high-margin iPhones. Moreover, the so-called iWallet could become a key selling feature and create yet another means to lock people into the iOS platform. The launch of the much-awaited iWallet and the prospect of innovative m-commerce apps built on top of Apple's mobile wallet hub could be the watershed event that would ultimately prompt merchants to upgrade their POS terminals to support NFC, and as a consequence, even competing mobile wallet platforms could benefit.

However, the industry hadn't settled on NFC as a standard yet. So, for the iPhone 5 launch in September 2012, Apple recognized the lack of demand and decided to forgo NFC to wait another cycle for the technology and infrastructure to develop further. Apparently, Apple had little incentive to push consumers in that direction. According to Phil Schiller, Apple's senior vice president, "It's not clear that NFC is the solution to any current problem." Here, he communicated a basic fact about NFC-based payments: they weren't universally accepted yet. The absence of NFC in the iPhone 5 feature list dealt a setback to the short-range wireless technology, which was still waiting for its Cinderella moment.

Apple, unlike Google, didn't come out and over promise and under deliver. The PC pioneer from California often bided its time before diving into developing technology markets, which explained why it was largely on the sidelines in the mobile-payment wars. According to Piper Jaffray analyst Gene Munster, Apple is always a comfortable number two, citing its relatively late entries in the MP3 player, smartphone and tablet markets as examples. "They let their competitors do their market research for them." When Apple embraced a technology it became obsessed with perfecting the whole value chain—and getting the value chain part was critical in the triumph of any m-commerce undertaking. Moreover, Apple was generally happy for other players to break new ground. The Cupertino, California–based company then came along with a user-friendly version and tried to win the lion's share of the market.

In the mobile payments arena, Apple didn't actually need to make any deals with banks or even the companies that manufactured card readers in stores for all this to work, as it already had a highly efficient system through which to carry out a transaction: iTunes. By 2012, Apple had roughly 400 million active accounts in iTunes, each with a valid credit card number. iTunes had become the envy of online retailers by creating a low-friction purchasing mechanism in which users gave Apple their credit card number when they signed up and they never had to pause to retrieve their wallet when they wanted to buy some service. That removed not only the physical barrier but some psychological barriers as well. Buying apps on Apple's App Store was super easy because the mobile user's credit card number was already in the device. To be in the App Store was like being part of a university club: they know who you are when you walk in and they have your billing information. No need to show your ID and no need to use cash in the club to pay the bills.

Apple's iOS mobile platform produced higher retention rates also because the company required developers to use its own payment system from day one. The fact that every single developer was using the Apple payment system was one of the things that helped Apple succeed in the mobile game.

Coming back to Apple's highly talked about foray into mobile payments domain, there was one piece in the iWallet puzzle: Apple had already incorporated in its iPhone 4S handsets the Bluetooth Low-Energy technology, which, much like the NFC tags, acted passively in the form of stickers and connected and transferred information seamlessly. The Bluetooth Low-Energy connection worked as far as 50 meters and could eventually enable payments-on-the-go without the need of fixed point-of-sale and traditional check-outs. And while NFC terminals were most likely be influenced by credit card companies, with Bluetooth Low-Energy stickers, it would all be done within the Apple world. The concept built around this ultra low-power technology solution complemented Apple's iTunes universe, circumvented the need for a register counter in Apple Stores, and sidestepped a direct confrontation with wireless operators.

Then, Apple took another step toward mobile payments when it introduced the Passbook app for iOS devices in 2012. Passbook aggregated a variety of consumer retail items such as digital coupons, stored-value cards, loyalty points, movie tickets and boarding passes into an easy-to-navigate app—just about everything related to a physical wallet except credit card transactions. Passbook was a purely software-based payment system; all an iPhone 5 user needed was a connection to the Internet through local Wi-Fi or cellular network. The Passbook app came with an open API, which was a departure for Apple and meant that gift cards issued by third parties like Starbucks could leap immediately into Passbook. The Apple-built app aggregated tickets, boarding passes, coupons and so forth from third-party apps like Sephora and Starbucks in one convenient place. Although an iPhone 5 user could use Passbook to make payments at some retailers, like Starbucks, its strength lied in quickly and easily displaying coupon, ticket codes or gift cards.

Passbook stored the items as barcodes which suited the Apple ecosystem in every way that NFC didn't. Unlike NFC, barcodes and barcode scanners were ubiquitous. So Passbook could set off the early adoption of mobile payments by advancing the idea of gift cards which had long transcended their initial purpose as gifts. Passbook let mobile users store a bigger stack of cards than their physical wallet ever could, so they could in theory carry around gift cards for most of the stores they frequented. By embracing gift cards, Apple was leveraging a decades-old infrastructure that provided a way to make mobile payments that nearly all consumers readily understood. Now a gift card was no more a gift card; it was a form of payments. A mobile user could link his credit card to his digital gift card and pay at the store with that instead of cash.

Apple had finally joined the mobile payments gold rush but some industry observers questioned what value Passbook brought in an already crowded arena of mobile payment apps, including Google Now which was based on scannable passes just like Passbook. They argued that Passbook should be more than simply an aggregator of digital cards and instead offer something truly unique. The iPhone 5 users must first download the brand's mobile app—like Starbucks and United Airlines—and then connect the app into Passbook. Some early users found this process confusing and duplicative given the manual work needed to add different cards and services into Passbook with limited return.

Apple didn't mention NFC support in Passbook, but some industry watchers were certain that Apple could eventually link Passbook to iTunes, allowing Apple to employ NFC as a mobile payment tool that could connect to its millions of iTunes accounts. That way, iTunes could evolve from a platform for buying apps and music to buying all kinds of things. So, paradoxically, going one step further, if Apple really wanted to disrupt the credit card companies, it could bypass them entirely, building its own online-payment infrastructure and offering discounts or other incentives to those who chose it for iTunes and other payments.

Apple had a huge cash stockpile to cobble the payment network infrastructure to work directly with banks. The Cupertino-based firm enjoyed a large developer community, and by incorporating an NFC chip into its devices, it could help spark the creation of a lot of new applications based on this short-distance technology. Apple could also find a lot of use for NFC in the non-payment arena, including transferring content between devices, obtaining local marketing offers from signposts, and physical entry into buildings. Moreover, Apple had a large network of physical stores that could serve as a showcase for the technology and as a classroom where people learned firsthand how to tap-and-go, and why they should consider using it. There were other good reasons for Apple to create its own iPay-style platform. The company, for instance, could expand its core hardware business with a new product line: POS terminals for millions of cafes, restaurants, and retail shops.

But payment was a complicated business and bypassing credit card companies was fraught with complexities and obstacles. Few companies had even bothered trying, PayPal being a notable exception. Others, like Google Wallet, were content on a front-end interface that let users plug into the incumbent credit giants. Apple would need to persuade many of its 400 million iTunes customers to trust it to handle payments for everyday purchases. Apple would also need to win the trust of retailers, even as iPads were starting to appear in retail storefronts. But most importantly, Apple would need to navigate the complex world of financial regulations, not just in the United States, but in every country where it offered iPay-like systems. It was also imperative for Apple to wait and see what the wireless carriers were willing to do. Moreover, as of 2013, there were still a lot of retail locations that weren't ready to handle NFC transactions.

The pre- and post-NFC worlds presented a rather complicated scenario. But if there was one company on the planet which had the potential to disrupt the credit card-centric payment system, it was Apple. If it ever made such a move, the consumer credit card could go the way of the digital camera or the GPS navigation device. Industry analysts widely believed that Apple would eventually come out swinging once consumers became more comfortable with substituting their phones for their wallets, and that Passbook was a precursor to iPay. Apple engineers mostly referred to Passbook as the "wallet app." Passbook was most likely an experiment to test consumer behavior around making non-iTunes transactions on iPhones.

Nevertheless, equipping the iPhone 5 with NFC would have been a huge education moment for consumers and a big validation for NFC. Developers could also get on board and create some really interesting apps with Apple's encouragement. Much of the industry was still counting on NFC. For instance, Samsung, Apple's archrival in the smartphone space, had introduced tectiles, programmable stickers that made NFC really easy for consumers to use even for non-payment applications. Apple had missed another iPhone cycle and it risked missing out on the learning curve and consumer feedback that could only be gained by working with the industry.

## THE NFC PARADOX

As of 2013, the mobile payment technology was far from reaching critical mass despite articles dating back years claiming this would be the "Year of NFC." The mobile payment ecosystem was still a confusing mess with half dozen competing solutions, a plethora of digital wallet apps, innumerable startups, banks, financial institutions, industry giants, wireless operators, regulators, POS hardware producers, joint ventures, and merchants all vying for a slice of what could be a very big pie. The mobile payment space was looking as fragmented as ever and was becoming more fragmented with every major announcement. Somewhere in the fray was the consumer, who by and large was standing on the sidelines, watching these entities play the payment game and waiting to see what solution would actually become ubiquitous enough to rely on. The consumer needed a universal and interoperable system but these companies continued to fight it out while leaving money on the table.

There were two fatal problems. First, the value proposition was weak. Why would a consumer care about shaving a few seconds off the time it took to swipe a card? The user experience of swiping plastic had been refined over the course of sixty years and it worked quite well. Second, the NFC-based tap-to-pay technology suffered a chicken and egg problem. Without widespread adoption by consumers, merchants had little reason to upgrade to the new technology. Without acceptance of a high proportion of merchants, consumers had little incentive to even try the technology. The challenge of the chicken and egg could be overcome, but it required a strong value proposition. That's where the fourth major stakeholder—apps and app developers— entered the fray. It was apparent by now that the real value hinged on innovative third-party apps plugged into the mobile wallet hub.

The NFC-based solutions offered thus far didn't solve a meaningful problem in the daily lives of consumers or merchants. Near field communication needed to provide real value for both consumers and merchants. The real value of NFC lied in a number of non-payment actions such as analytics, loyalty schemes, and related systems like transportation tickets. It was a much bigger space. So the key was not in payments but the features layered on top that would allure both consumers and merchants: discounts, daily deals, and loyalty reward programs activated through NFC technology. If people used their phones to pay for items, check in at stores for coupons and grab deals from NFC-embedded posters and use them for discounts, it could provide critical data to retailers, helping them craft offers for mobile users, track sales, and change their product lineups. More customer data would help merchants strengthen their relationships with consumers by allowing them to embed loyalty cards into mobile wallets. Near field communication would then become more of an exchange of discounts and deals rather than a mere cash replacement.

Clearly, there were a lot of other NFC uses outside the payments realm. A customer tapped his mobile phone on the doorway of a store and exposed his commerce identity to the retailer: a first-time customer, a loyal customer, a brand-conscious customer, a budget customer, and so on. The retailer could quickly work out a complete personalization around the offers, deals and information for that specific customer. It was also plausible that NFC would find other uses first; for instance, allowing people to unlock their houses and not worry about keys anymore. It would be safe to say, therefore, that the real power of tapping a phone was in mobile shopping and convenience use cases rather than mere mobile payments. The bright spots in the guise of new apps mentioned above could actually prepare consumers for contactless payments through NFC mechanism.

Take the example of Korean smartphone maker Samsung who pioneered a new way to champion the short-distance wireless technology when it introduced programmable tags on NFC-enabled Android devices. These tags, which responded to a series of commands to perform repetitive tasks, were a testament that NFC could work in a variety of non-payment settings. Mobile users could tap the back of their phone against a tectile tag to check in at a location, open a map, swap business contact information, or "like" something. The tags, sold by wireless operators, would work with a free tectile app, downloadable through Google Play, and the app would allow users to program the NFC tags as many times as needed. An NFC tag use case: mobile consumers using an NFC-enabled smartphone or other NFC device could read an electric meter and securely transmit usage information to a utility for payment.

The notion of an NFC-centric mobile wallet wasn't merely about phasing out plastic; it was about extending beyond plastic. The mobile wallet wasn't bound to be limited to credit card-like uses. Replacing a plastic device with a smartphone or a tablet capable of receiving as well as sending a variety of information in a visual manner fundamentally changed the whole shopping experience. The mobile wallet could close the loop to connect specific marketing campaigns with in-store results, and at the same time, be a channel for promotions to drive people into the store. Then there were account management and alerts that the mobile wallet could facilitate by informing mobile users at any time about the current balance or how much credit was still available. The mobile wallet, hooked to a bank account or the PayPal app, could also serve as a seamless mechanism for money transfer. Peer-to-peer NFC use-cases like money transfer could become more frequent as consumers became more familiar with the technology.

The new payment paradigm could also facilitate expense and receipt tracking through innovative new apps. Another bright spot: Stagecoach, a national bus operator in Britain, was conceiving an NFC ticketing system in partnership with mobile operator Everything Everywhere. Another use case allowed drivers to wave or tap their NFC-enabled phones over the NFC sticker on the parking meter to automatically launch the parking application. The mobile payment system recognized the user, identified the individual parking location and the driver entered the desired parking time to complete the transaction. The system then sent a text message reminder before the parking period expired and, if needed, allowed additional time to be purchased by phone. A receipt was automatically sent to the user's e-mail account. Payment was processed against a credit or debit card associated with the mobile phone number. The NFC sticker had a passive electronic chip that didn't require a battery and stored information such as the parking space number that could be read wirelessly by any NFC-enabled phone.

Marketers and technologists alike had pined for the era when the mobile phone would become our wallet. But these were still very early days for mobile payments industry. Consumers had no big issues with credit cards and paying for something with mobile phone was still a new concept for the masses.

Nearly 85 percent of commerce still involved cash and checks. A 2012 study from comScore on mobile wallets found that the only digital payment service more than half of Americans had ever heard of was PayPal. Only 41 percent of those polled had heard of Google Wallet, while a mere 8 percent had ever used Google's service. Isis scored far lower, with only 6 percent familiar with the platform and only 1 percent having ever used it.

A mobile payments platform should be simple and super convenient. On the contrary, mobile payments were a complex process. Mobile wallet-based payment systems needed to weed out operation- and security-related problems and ensure that the systems worked smoothly to communicate a clear message that mobile payments were real and had value. Case in point: Square alone had increased the number of credit-card readers in the United States by about a sixth. Some 26 million small businesses and self-employed people in America had wanted to accept card payments but were put off by the cost and the paperwork. A traditional card-reader sold for hundreds of dollars, with fixed monthly fees on top, and applicants had to submit to credit checks and provide accounts for the previous year.

Near-field communications had been around since early 2000s. By 2013, however, NFC technology started to break out of its shell. The early momentum for mobile payments would not have been possible without the massive growth in the number of smartphones and the falling cost of computing power, both of which were lowering the barriers to new entrants in parts of the financial industry. While this chapter encompassed much of the efforts from the technology industry in the making of the mobile wallet, the next chapter will focus on initiatives from the financial industry and try to connect the dots to make sense of this whole mobile wallet thing. For the "anytime, anywhere" mantra of mobile retail, it was imperative that banking and financial industries joined hands with technology outfits to make mobile shopping a seamless consumer experience.

# 5 BATTLE OF THE MOBILE WALLETS

*"There won't be mass adoption of mobile payments until there is a better consumer experience beyond the card."*

— Jennifer Schulz, head of global product strategy at Visa

Smartphones equipped with powerful new apps were unmistakably reinvigorating the long-held promise of m-banking services. A growing number of businesses were eyeing mobile payments as an alternative to credit cards. Such a move would presumably reduce costs to merchants, who were typically charged 3 percent of the purchase price when customers paid with a credit card. In the early euphoria of possibilities that NFC created, technology pundits said that the mobile phone was smart while credit cards were dumb and a mere piece of plastic. They also perceived banks as risk-averse and technology laggards. They saw the use of NFC for payments as part of a larger surge in mobile payment alternatives to credit cards and paper tickets. Then there were use cases such as money transfer, online banking, physical good sales, and coupons.

Just like wireless networks and their operators, banks were seen as in danger of becoming the dumb pipes in the quickly evolving mobile payment realm. In the traditional setup, banks served a purpose: Hold onto people's money, loan it to them at times and protect it from bad guys. Now the evolution of currency in the digital domain brought many questions marks about the future of banks. On the flip side, however, the banks had a say in how smartphone payment scheme would work. Banks had millions of customers, existing merchant relationships, and most of the money in the world. So they were likely to remain a necessary back-end component in any mobile wallet initiative. Moreover, consumers trusted financial services institutions to handle transactions and would more likely embrace mobile payments once they saw financial institutions like banks and credit card companies were involved in the mobile payment value chain. Not surprisingly, therefore, all the major mobile payment initiatives were aligned with banks and credit card companies.

Credit cards had a long and distinguished history. In 1950, the Diners Club issued a credit card for paying restaurant bills. Soon after that credit cards emerged as dining cards and quickly became a fashionable item among the rich and famous of Manhattan. But the real breakthrough came in 1958, when a Bank of America manager named Joe Williams sent nearly all 60,000 households in Fresno, California a new credit card, without even asking that they fill out an application or submit to a credit check. The Great Fresno Drop, as it was later called, also persuaded some 1,000 retailers in the area to embrace this new form of payment. Although fraud was rampant and felonious accounts were prevalent, within two years, the cards had spread throughout California. In the next decade, these plastic cards spread across the United States introducing the era of electronic money. Credit card companies benefited as people abandoned cash and paper checks for cards and electronic payments. The era of plastic had kick-started.

Fast forward to 2010, Visa and MasterCard accounted for US$2.45 trillion of consumer spending on credit and debit cards in the United States. Merchants paid an estimated US$2 trillion annually as interchange fee—the toll charge paid to credit card companies for processing transactions. And credit card companies did more than just facilitate purchases; they handled big-time lending and loan business amounting to as much as US$6 billion a year. Now, amid shifting tides, when smartphones could potentially displace some of the 1 billion credit and debit cards in American wallets, credit card firms began exploring what could be the future of commerce: quick and efficient payment processing through mobile technology. Evidently, the giant card payment networks—American Express, Discover, MasterCard and Visa—wanted to move aggressively into the emerging mobile payments industry, but couldn't do so without significantly disrupting their existing business models.

Seeing the forces of disruption at their doorsteps, credit card companies spent millions of dollars to issue new cards with contactless NFC technology and vowed to speed up the check-out process. Credit card companies had been toying with the NFC concept for quite some time by embedding the technology into credit cards and thus allowing their customers to wave a card in front of a reader instead of using the traditional swipe method. As to the future, senior executives from credit card companies argued that NFC was merely a wireless mechanism to process a transaction, and ultimately it would come down to creating a viable payment infrastructure that took care of how money moved, ensured that transactions worked every time, and preserved legal rights for consumers, merchants, and banks.

Nevertheless, it was refreshing to see that the long-established financial institutions were being relatively open minded and innovative in pushing a technology that ultimately promised to benefit all. The fact that MasterCard joined hands with European operator Deutsche Telekom for an NFC wallet service was a sign of how credit card companies realized they had to team up with wireless companies and set a beachhead against mobile payment insurgencies from smartphone makers and smaller outfits like Square. By being open with all stakeholders in the payment value chain, including wireless operators and mobile phone makers, credit card companies were also contributing to make the process frictionless. In a way, they were playing Switzerland in all of this: Confident in their financial strengths and trying to remain impartial when they were approached by anyone to promote NFC technology.

Evidently, by being active on the wireless front and taking the central role of a facilitator for everything from helping to standardize payment security to developing technology for merchants, the masters of the plastic card payment paradigm wanted to cement their own stakes in the next generation of payment systems. The fact of the matter was that smartphone-based payment technologies were actually boosting usage of credit cards. Companies like Square and PayPal had developed tiny card readers that plugged into smartphones and allowed small traders to accept payments cheaply through mobile apps that required users to enter their credit card details.

## PLASTIC VERSUS PHONE

The rise of the mobile wallet marked a neutral ground for banks and credit card firms, but there could be winners and losers among them as well. It was apparent by now that the credit card companies were looking beyond their traditional products and were stepping up with their own digital payment services that were more open, mobile and cross-channel. While technology companies were trying to redefine payments in a more mobile and social context, the credit card companies were making sure they didn't fall behind and lose their relationship with consumers. The credit card firms seemed to have a pivotal role in the mobile payments juggernaut also because they had exceptionally strong brands and a trusted relationship with consumers. Credit card companies, for instance, could play a crucial role in the evolution of mobile payments by equipping retailers with new POS terminals as the entry point for consumers. Moreover, they could more effectively provide retailers with services like data analytics and promotion services.

So while credit card firms showcased their own wallet and payment solutions, their strategy in the mobile payments realm was more or less the same: they allowed their banking systems to be plugged into tech industry initiatives like Isis, but at the same time, they were making the case for their mobile wallet products as well. Take American Express which started out in the Nineteen Century delivering money on horseback and issued the first widely accepted plastic charge card in 1959. Fast forward to 2012, its digital payments and commerce platform—Serve—integrated a variety of payment options into a single account that could be funded by a bank account, debit, or credit card.

The Serve digital platform, which enabled online transactions, peer-to-peer payments and carrier billing through Payfone, became a bit like a mobile wallet within a wallet when integrated into the Isis payment system. Serve was partly an Internet service and partly a debit card. Not only was the service free, new customers were being offered a US$10 credit to get started. It was the New York–based finance giant's first product designed for the Internet and smartphones, and it aimed to compete directly with PayPal. And it wasn't just American Express flaunting its digital wallet service; other companies were also clamoring to become the credit card of choice for digital transactions. Visa touted its own payment and wallet solutions—payWave NFC payment system, V.me, and Visa Mobile Prepay—to obviate the need for Isis platform.

Visa's digital payments service V.me aimed to make it easier for consumers to shop online, whether via desktop web, mobile phone or tablet computer. The service was effectively a digital wallet, which stored not only Visa card information, but also MasterCard, American Express and Discover cards. When a consumer was on a supported merchant's website, instead of entering in his payment information and shipping preferences manually, he only had to enter in his e-mail and password. The merchant still received payment through Visa's network, but the consumer's 16-digit card number was not displayed on the site, adding another layer of security to the transaction. It's worthwhile to note that a digital wallet wasn't necessarily the same as a "mobile wallet," although a digital wallet service could also be packaged into a mobile wallet app and vice versa.

Visa, while acknowledging NFC as the best chance for mobile payment acceptance in the short term, believed that more and more of payment activities would eventually happen in the cloud without any physical interaction. So the credit card giant planned to introduce a mobile payments element to its digital wallet service and leverage NFC and QR codes to allow consumers to tap their phone to a secure reader at the point of sale or scan a QR code in order to pay for purchases. MasterCard, too, had its own take on digital wallet. It was, however, pursuing a more open approach and was amenable to working with partners instead of owning every piece of the mobile payment stack. By doing so MasterCard was putting more of its effort into broad partnerships, so no matter who came out on top, it would be there.

MasterCard was expanding its mobile payment service PayPass into a larger platform called PayPass Wallet Services which would enable PayPal-like online payments and would include software tools for developers to integrate their payment apps and services into PayPass and take advantage of MasterCard's check-out, authentication, and security services. PayPass Wallet gave consumers a way to pay for things using any brand of credit, debit and pre-paid cards—Visa, American Express, Discover, etc.—while consumers would be able to easily check out without having to enter in credit card and shipping information. PayPass also offered a host of features for consumers such as quick balance checking before purchases, spending controls, alerts received in real-time, personalized offers, and loyalty programs.

In the end, what was needed to make NFC payments work was a handset that was enabled, a merchant that was enabled, a bank that had given its permission, a mobile operator who had given access to its network, a trusted manager in the middle, and a willing consumer. The Google Wallet project was a testament that it wasn't enough to just push out a new mobile wallet technology. All major players in the mobile payment value chain would need to address the trust issue. Mobile users would need to be assured they could trust their smartphones and the mobile payment systems to be as secure as their existing options. Then, there were perceived data security and privacy issues that could hold back mobile payments' early momentum. Whoever mastered the privacy challenge would gain a significant competitive edge in the m-commerce space.

## PAYPAL GOES MOBILE

A lot of companies were trying to get their arms around mobile payments. These companies were now in a race to get merchants to install software onto their check-out terminals, so that their wallets could manage sending advertisements and loyalty points to mobile customers. PayPal, a prominent m-commerce market contender, had a myriad of NFC and non-NFC solutions to leverage its hundred million plus credit card subscribers. PayPal had demonstrated that mobile—both for online and offline payments—was where it saw its future. The eBay subsidiary made its mark in online payments, but saw a much bigger opportunity in targeting around 85 percent of transactions that still happened in physical retail stores. For that, PayPal had to get more mobile.

First, there came PayPal Here—a Square-like mobile payments platform for small businesses—which comprised of a tiny card reader designed to plug into the headphone jack of an iOS or Android device. The triangle-shaped credit card reader that plugged into a smartphone was aimed at a wide range of street-based vendors and other small businesses that wanted to expand their payment options but weren't large enough to justify the expense of a mobile POS machine. If a mobile user wanted to pay by credit card, the card was swiped through the reader and then the customer signed the screen with his finger. The system could even send him a receipt if needed. PayPal would charge 2.7 percent on transactions, just under the 2.75 percent that Square charged. Mobile card readers like Square and PayPal Here proved more popular with both merchants and consumers, albeit in the short-term, because they used smartphones instead of traditional card readers to process transactions and didn't require a new learning curve. These solutions didn't require merchants to invest a significant amount in new technology, like replacing existing POS systems with NFC-enabled machines.

Both Square and PayPal Here also supported merchant-friendly services like real-time location-based ads, coupons, loyalty points, and in-store deals. For PayPal, time was the essence to make a massive land grab against agile startups like Square and beat them in their own game through sheer power of scale. Shaving a little off the transaction fee was always nice for the merchants. Moreover, merchants could get 1 percent off on transactions using a PayPal debit card that pulled money from a PayPal account. While leaving their money there gave instant access to merchants, it also assumed that merchants wanted to keep their money inside a PayPal account instead of moving it to a bank account, a process which could take one to three days. Square, on the other hand, deposited the transaction amount directly into a merchant's bank account.

Concurrently, the eBay-owned company offered a cloud-based NFC alternative that allowed customers to pay for products by using their phones to scan barcodes or by entering their mobile number and a PIN code at existing payment terminals. PayPal's mobile wallet platform worked through a smartphone app or a PayPal card, or even a phone number and PIN that held a consumer's information from credit and debit cards from multiple providers. The system relied on integrating PayPal software into existing POS terminals so customers could pay either by swiping a PayPal pre-paid card or by entering their phone number and PIN, which seamlessly connected to their account. PayPal had also built in the geo-fencing technology in the product so mobile users could notify a store they were on their way or inside a store and check out without having to go to the counter.

PayPal as an online payment and money transfer service also allowed people to send money via e-mail, phone, text message or Skype. The PayPal Mobile service leveraged the e-commerce stalwart's ability to effortlessly connect its customers to bank accounts and credit cards, and allowed users to send payments by text message or by using PayPal's mobile browser. Then there was PayPal's dongle solution, which along with an app for merchants that allowed them to take PayPal payments via a phone number, could win merchants interested in tapping PayPal's existing customer base. The dongle and accompanying app for merchants also revealed PayPal's larger ambitions to take its online payments forte to the physical world.

As of 2012, PayPal was one of the world's leading digital payment platforms with 100 million plus users and US$145 billion worth of annual transactions. But the relationships with physical stores still weren't a strong suit for PayPal and a late start put PayPal at a slight disadvantage. So PayPal was hard at work with its novel in-store payment tricks for big-box retailers, which had been adopted by Home Depot first as a five-store pilot and then within two months at its 2,000 locations across the United States. Then fifteen U.S. retailers—including Barnes & Noble, JC Penny, Office Depot and Nine West—followed this brick-and-mortar rollout. PayPal, now more determined than ever to capture share in the burgeoning mobile payments markets, had won a long list of retailers to build its market share through an alternate payment system. It was also joining hands with POS equipment makers like Verifone so that PayPal's mobile payment solutions could be integrated into their terminals through simple software upgrades.

Then there was PayPal inStore feature, which worked by displaying a barcode on the smartphone's screen, which was scanned by the traditional cash-register barcode reader. The clerk simply scanned the mobile phone instead of swiping a credit card through a reader. The next stop in PayPal's all-out offensive in mobile and local payment systems: the acquisition of startup card.io which worked with iOS and Android developers to help them integrate mobile credit and debit card payment capabilities into their apps without the need of additional hardware like Square's card reader. Instead, card.io's partners used the phone's built-in camera to snap a photo of a credit card. The card number and related information was extracted and passed to a payment processor to complete the transaction. It was likely that PayPal could eventually replace its own card reader hardware for card.io's innovative payment solution.

In 2012 consumer surveys, PayPal showed up as the most popular choice amongst those interested in using a mobile wallet. PayPal with its cross-ecosystem approach was arguably the world's biggest bank with more than 100 million account holders. PayPal, like Square, was among the earliest contenders to seize on a market opportunity that major credit-card companies and traditional commerce and technology players largely missed. And like Square, PayPal required little effort on the user's part, but offered high value in return. Moreover, PayPal built on something most people were already using— its e-commerce service—and added the critical element of security and privacy. Consumers didn't give out their financial details to merchants or sellers because they were secure inside the PayPal account.

## MOBILE WALLET MAKEOVER

Paying by SMS for items like ringtones started back in the late 1990s and the concept of using a phone as a wallet emerged in 2004 when NFC made its debut on mobile handsets. Next, in the post-iPhone period, major players began marshaling their forces by forging partnerships and establishing technology baselines. By 2011, they started deploying innovations in the larger ecosystem while testing the market to see how it would react. Industry experts following the mobile payments market had originally projected that NFC would become an industry standard in 2012. But it would take a while in the buildup of a robust payment network through smartphones. While NFC was seemingly primed to become the underlying technology for mobile payment systems, the battle for the control of the mobile wallet wouldn't be over anytime soon. The m-commerce game had just started.

It was a settling-in period for NFC technology platform. The technology and financial sectors were moving forward to create the infrastructure that would make mobile payments realistic for buying physical goods at the point of sale. A key stumbling block: The NFC-based payment standard required merchants to change their POS terminals and thus carry out both hardware and software upgrades; merchants had already installed thousands of Visa payWave and MasterCard PayPass terminals. So ultimately it was merchants who would figure out the best options among payment solutions provided by technology and financial companies. Until there was a critical mass for such a standard to emerge, there might not be enough retailers to adopt NFC gear. Besides NFC, a group of industry observers also counted beam technologies and QR codes as candidates for POS integration as they also brought some unique value to the transaction process.

To make things more challenging, merchants were too self involved to bring about any tangible change. Some merchants even launched their own mobile-money platforms to lure consumers. If merchants like Starbucks gained enough traction, payment solutions like these could circumvent banks, credit card companies, and the wireless industry altogether. As of 2013, the largest mobile payment program in the United States was run by Starbucks coffee shops. Merchants like Starbucks were the wild card in the mobile payments game. They had an enormous amount at stake. The credit card services interchange came out of their bottom line and they were the ones who would pay for the ads and promotions linked to the mobile wallet. Moreover, the cost of upgrading the NFC payment terminals to accept tap-to-pay was going to be borne by the merchants.

Not surprisingly, therefore, some merchants wanted to steer more spending to private label stored-value cards and avoid interchange fees altogether. That way, a merchant would retain its own data to support customer loyalty programs, rather than enabling media giants like Google to target competitor ads to that merchant's customers. That eventually led the large retailers—already hit hard by Amazon—to collaborate on creating their own mobile wallet solution. Walmart, Target and several other large retailers decided to work on their own mobile payment system that would compete against the likes of Google Wallet, Isis, PayPal, and others. The companies involved in this initiative—big-box retailers, fast-food restaurants, drug stores and vending companies— had combined annual revenues of US$1.38 trillion.

It was a huge pile of money that big retail shops wanted to defend from the salivating technology and financial services industries. Furthermore, retailers already had to deal with a lot of middlemen and they weren't very keen about sharing revenue and data with outsiders. But initiatives like this could throw the nascent mobile payment market into even more chaos and make it harder for consumers to decide which mobile wallet they were supposed to carry in their phones.

Inevitably, there was going to be some confusion in the short term for consumers as well as for merchants who would have to contemplate hardware upgrades to take advantage of NFC's contactless payment abilities. The confusion over competing NFC efforts that didn't interoperate could also hold back early adoption. It was the early going and none of the stakeholders wanted to give up the chance to dominate the entire mobile payment space. But, eventually, it was expected that all the major stakeholders would find a way to shake hands, interoperate, and make life easier for the consumer. A harbinger of this premise was the fact that while payments using NFC had barely gotten off the ground, it was still seen as headed toward a bright future. A predominant part of the industry was preparing for an NFC-centric payment future. The world was on the verge of one of the biggest changes in decades in how people paid for goods and services.

No payment system was useful unless it was widely accepted. So, in the midst of a confusing picture, in August 2012, came the inevitable. The four top U.S. wireless carriers—Verizon, AT&T, Sprint and T-Mobile—as well as Google, Isis, PayPal, VeriFone, and Intuit joined hands to form the Mobile Payments Committee within the umbrella of the trade body Electronic Transactions Association. The goal of the committee would be to help guide legislators and regulators on mobile payment public policy, sort out the different business relationships between the members, and work on education for consumers and merchants. It was just a committee and it would most likely work in a slow fashion like other committees. Still, it symbolized a sense of admission from key players of the mobile payment game that in-fighting was holding them back and that confusion among consumers and merchants was in nobody's interest.

The NFC technology promised the power to change pretty much everything from the way people shopped, to the way they exchanged information with other phone owners, advertising, and so on. The impetus for this landmark shift could also come from the fact that smartphones were becoming more commonplace by the day. Eighty-five percent of the world's transactions were still made with cash and checks, and smartphones, with economy of scale on their side, could shift much of this to the digital domain. The availability of NFC-enabled smartphones would inevitably provide a boost for the mobile wallet that benefited everyone by promising to replace a host of cards, coins and cash. The smartphone would not only become a mobile user's wallet, the device would also serve as a portal for access to multiple accounts and apps. The integration of location-based services and coupons would also motivate users to begin adopting NFC technology. Moreover, having NFC support meant cutting out all steps that came with apps like Foursquare—launch an app, activate check-in, etc.—and just tap the phone to use that app.

Society had already transitioned from holding their own money to trusting banks, and eventually, to trusting credit card companies for buying goods. Now technology firms and financial institutions were joining hands to create an even more convenient way to spend money through a new era of currency embedded into a smartphone. But the evolution of currency wasn't something that would happen overnight. The mobile payments adoption depended on a variety of factors, from infrastructure deployment to standard technology to consumer willingness to make payments with a mobile device. The first evolution of digital currency occurred when banks and credit card companies put debit and credit cards in the hand of consumers and card readers at retail locations. The infrastructure needed to change that mode of transactions was being built gradually.

The right infrastructure was clearly the starting point. After infrastructure, security was probably the most critical entity within the payments value chain. The security implications raised too many concerns about the safety of the money. So it was imperative for an NFC-enabled smartphone to transform itself into an authentication device to facilitate transactions at check-out places. Chapter 11 will delve into security-related issues in more detail. Furthermore, the overall process in mobile payments didn't happen as smoothly as laid out in business plans. The payment industry still had a long way to go to create a seamless mobile experience for consumers. Mobile payment, for instance, was rarely coordinated across multiple channels—e-mail, SMS, push notifications, Passbook, and mobile ads—to create a positive experience for mobile users and point-of-sale.

And finally, the new payments paradigm needed to be as frictionless as possible. As exemplified in the e-commerce world by stalwarts like Amazon, nothing beat the one-click check-out experience for digital shoppers. The more steps merchants put between the consumer and the final trans-action, the more they risked consumers dropping off. It was significantly more cumbersome to enter credit card data on a mobile device. Speed also mattered in the limited band-width environment of the mobile world, so if merchants didn't optimize the process for the mobile environment, they were likely to lose sales due to a slow and painful experience that consumers just didn't have patience for. The consumer wasn't likely to wait a very long time for the transaction to complete and could abandon the purchase if the payment process didn't comprise of a single, efficient round-trip to the server to complete the purchase. That's why a predominant majority of consumers was likely to gravitate toward a single mobile wallet solution. Consumers would go with what was easy, what was trusted, what was convenient, and what gave them the most value.

In the end, despite severe pain points for both consumers and merchants, m-commerce was ramping up, proving that con-sumers still liked to shop via their mobile device. The surveys conducted in 2012 established that consumers placed significant value on the benefits of various offers and incentives, from lower interest rates and cash back rewards to discounts and sales coordinated with loyalty programs. The techno shoppers were mostly attracted to the shopping and social features of mobile wallets while payment optimizers were interested in making the best payment decisions based on their financial situation, loyalty benefits, and account management. At the same time, however, the numbers showed that there was significant room for improvement in the mobile purchasing experience—mainly through optimizing the shopping and payment processes for consumers.

There were four major types of mobile payment solutions that mattered: carrier billing, short-range wireless or NFC, apps, and card readers. Chapters 4 and 5 provided a detailed treatment of NFC- and apps-centric payment modes. Mobile users were increasingly utilizing apps on their smartphones to pay, typically by scanning a barcode at the register. Card readers, piggybacked on the existing credit card network, pioneered by Square, have been discussed in the prologue of this book. In carrier billing, the oldest and most entrenched payment method, mobile phone users paid by text message and the charge was added to their phone bill. The payment solution was highly practical for a variety of specific use cases and could reach consumers not affiliated with banks, like teenagers, but was crimped by wireless carrier fees and control. Chapter 11 briefly delves into this specific payment mode and attempts to chart future trends.

That concludes this book's coverage of the mobile payment industry, one of fundamental building blocks of the mobile commerce juggernaut. Here, it'd be worthwhile to mention bellwether mobile payment startups like LevelUp which didn't charge an interchange fee for every payment consumers made and instead made money by offering deals to consumers within the app. Mobile users earned additional credit as they spent repeatedly at the same merchant—the digital version of loyalty punch card. It was a testament that mobile commerce was increasingly becoming a converged world. In fact, LevelUp was following an advertising and data business model that could eventually become central to the future of mobile payments.

The next chapter will delve into the "location" building block and how it was transforming the m-commerce industry at large. It kicks off with the case study of a financial services company—Green Dot—who was reinventing itself by acquiring the location assets of a Silicon Valley startup, Loopt.

# 6 WHEN LOCATION MET COMMERCE

*"Location and granular geo-targeting are actually strong predictors of consumer intent— because where someone is and when they are there says a lot about what they might be interested in."*

— Alistair Goodman, CEO, Placecast

The acquisition of pioneer location app Loopt by the provider of retailer pre-paid cards Green Dot reinforced the unique combination of location and commerce. Loopt— founded in 2005 by Stanford University undergraduate Sam Altman—was one of the early location services which helped friends find each other through location tracking. It later helped users find better deals and get tips on venues but was eventually overshadowed by a far more powerful service from

Foursquare. The confluence of information about the users and where they go to match them up with retailers caught the eyes of Green Dot, who had relationships with businesses large and small. Green Dot enjoyed the stature of a bank, owned call centers and payment processing infrastructure, and carried all the other components for handling transactions on a larger scale.

Green Dot, headquartered outside Los Angeles, was founded in 1999 by Steve Streit, a former radio industry executive who originally aimed the service at teenage shoppers. Green Dot's product was a prepaid debit card; it looked and acted just like regular Visa or MasterCard plastic, but it must be funded by the owner before it could be used. While prepaid debit cards were becoming increasingly popular even for traditional banks, Green Dot stood out because it had built a huge retail network of nearly 50,000 locations, including 7-Eleven, Kmart, and Walgreens stores. Green Dot was a classic example of a new breed of financial-services company which used extremely sophisticated technology to target a singularly unpromising demographic: the estimated 60 million American considered "underbanked." Some of these millions subsisted at poverty level; many others simply couldn't afford the increasingly stiff monthly charges associated with traditional checking accounts.

The Loopt purchase represented an effort to establish a beachhead in the booming but competitive field of mobile-phone payments. Greet Dot—with a robust enterprise-level financial services infrastructure and retail POS financial transactions capability across the United States—could use Loopt to launch merchant deals on a local scale. It could use Loopt for a number of things like improving customer acquisition, retention of its prepaid debit cards, and driving adoption of new banking and payment products. Loopt could also help Green Dot become a player in the mobile wallet and rewards market for retailers.

The Greet Dot-Loopt rendezvous was a harbinger of how the banking and payments industry could be reshaped in a way that would be better for everyone. The deal was also a testament to the common belief that almost everything in the future would come through the device people held in their hands. Ultimately, it was mobile devices which offered the potential to change the way people interact with their banks, control their money, and pay for goods and services. Green Dot being a large-scale player in the retail POS business was buying intellectual property for location-based mobile marketing and messaging services in a bid to reinvent itself in the mobile arena.

As of 2013, the location technology was still outside the consciousness of mainstream consumers. While location-based services were trying to break into the mainstream in a lot of ways, many of these startups pushing the edge were being acquired by larger players. Loopt was just one example. Clearly, it would require a lot more effort from popular applications like Foursquare to make a difference on their own. For a start, the Foursquare app would now be able to read NFC tags at a location and immediately take the users to a venue page where they could check in. Near field communication opened up the opportunity for location-centric upstarts like Foursquare to become an even more integral tool for merchants. The location company, for instance, added support for restaurant menus; the app could function from each table with an NFC tag.

Next up, Foursquare could add an option for consumers to pay from tableside by using NFC tags or QR codes. The Internet's premier location services like Foursquare and NFC technology could help each other grow and mature. For NFC industry to make an impact and accomplish mass market appeal, NFC ports needed to get to more phones and to more locations. Here, outfits such as Foursquare could ultimately provide a long-overdue boost for NFC products. But that was easier said than done. Foursquare would have to first figure out how to get NFC tags out to thousands of merchants.

It was evident that location was a crucial element in the emerging world of mobile commerce. Once location joined hands with other critical building blocks of the mobile com- merce industry, the ecosystem would consolidate and win proponents both on consumer and business sides. This chap- ter attempts to provide a detailed treatment of the different facets of location technology, and see how this landmark technology fits into the bigger m-commerce landscape.

## QR CODES FOR STARTERS

A critical aspect of the m-commerce value chain was to keep it simple for local merchants whether they were retailers or restaurant owners. They should be the ones to choose deals or offer discounts, set their own terms, and track the ROI of their campaigns. Moreover, m-commerce solutions available to retailers mostly rewarded people who were already in the store. To simplify m-commerce solutions and find new ways to drive people into the store while taking advantage of social media channels, New York City–based Social Passport allowed merchants to post NFC tags or QR codes from their stores which mobile users could interact with to unlock deals, discounts and rewards. Social Passport, founded in October 2011, offered a social loyalty tool that leveraged both NFC and QR codes to allow mobile users to interact with their favorite stores in real-time and receive discounts, and in turn, give these businesses access to a wider audience of potential customers through their social media networks.

Mobile users could simply download the Social Passport app and start liking, following and checking in at their favorite stores, receiving deals tailored for them based on their inter-action with that store and in accordance with their social media footprints. On the other hand, merchants were able to take advantage of the viral potential of a few positive words from mobile users and reward them accordingly. A mobile phone user, for instance, might enter a store which had posted a QR code; the user scanned the code with Social Passport and found on his mobile phone screen a range of prompts offered by the store owner. The offers might ask the user to check in on Foursquare; post his location to Facebook; or follow or tweet his response on Twitter. After doing that the mobile user would be able to unlock deals, discounts and rewards offered by the store.

That way, business owners could strengthen their relationship with consumers using NFC tags and QR codes and could also incentivize people to share about a business through their social networks. Merchants, through their own dashboard, could set their deals and view analytics such as how many scans they accomplished, how many people they reached on social media channels, or how many people clicked on a specific message. The Social Passport platform also offered businesses their own custom QR and NFC stickers and punch-card features. If mobile users didn't have an NFC-enabled device, they could use both QR codes and reverse QR, the latter allowing users to display their own stickers which merchants could scan.

LevelUp was another prominent case study which created traction at the bottom of the market as a small mobile payments provider. The Boston–based startup provided QR-code-based payments for local merchants by allowing businesses to use Android phones as scanners that processed payments utilizing the LevelUp app. By 2013, 1 million people had signed up for the app, which displayed a debit or credit card-linked QR code that scanned as payment at nearly 5,000 merchants. Eventually, LevelUp evolved from an app that made payments to a platform that provided payment capabilities.

A quick response or QR code was a trackable two-dimensional matrix barcode that could be read by camera-equipped smartphones with the use of a simple QR app reader downloadable for free. They were souped-up versions of the barcode that could be embedded with a URL address, data, or text message. The QR reader decoded the code and the mobile user was instantly sent to a website, landing page, video, or social networking site. When scanned by a smartphone, these codes led mobile users to a store with a value proposition: deal, coupon or loyalty points. A QR code could be placed just about anywhere—printed advertisements in newspapers, yard signs, business cards, point-of-sale displays, etc. That way, QR codes allowed mobile users to interact with their environment twenty four hours a day.

Quick response codes were invented by Toyota subsidiary Denso Wave in 1994 as a tracking device for the car manufacturing industry. While they had been popular in Japan for several years, more than a decade after their inception, QR codes finally made their way to the United States, where they were now becoming more familiar and more popular for commerce purposes. Impulse-buying products—such as books, computer software and video games, music, videos and DVDs, and event tickets—required little intensive research, so QR codes could drive a significant portion of mobile retail sales.

The case studies relating to Social Passport and LevelUp just showed how location-aware and context-relevant shopping and payments experiences could radically transform the consumer behavior. Mobile users were increasingly showing a willingness to not only scan these codes, but shop with them too. However, the location-based experiences could revolutionize more than just shopping. QR codes were a location-centric bright spot also because they merged traditional in-person advertising with the mobile world through scannable bar code images that took a smartphone user to a particular website or downloadable piece of content.

In 2012, as much as 50 percent of smartphone users had been estimated to have scanned QR codes and 18 percent of them made a purchase after scanning. Quick response or QR codes were one of those mobile marketing channels that pleased everyone involved in the sale cycle—retailers because they connected consumers without their actual presence, consumers because they provided relevant information quickly, and marketers because they could be creatively placed. And they were free. Google's URL shortener could create a QR code. Free codes could also be produced at sources like Qurify or Kaywa. Quick response codes were great a way of driving traffic to business websites, however, they must be part of an integrated inbound strategy.

Indoor navigation startup aisle411 was another important case study for greater understanding of mobile buying behaviors and the evolution of mobile buyers. The company snagged its biggest retail partner in the Walgreens chain when its scaled in-store search solution allowed people to view the maps of any Walgreens store to locate products by aisle and section. The aisle411 app also supported other shopper-friendly functions like product listings, voice-to-text, and barcode scanning. However, aisle411's barcode scanning feature was designed to help customers add products to shopping lists, not to comparison shop for better prices—like those they could find on Amazon.com. So instead of closing the app, re-opening another app and then scanning products in search of deals and discounts, customers would find the product they wanted in the store, navigate there, and buy it. Walgreens' own app offered product listings, pharmacy access, refills by scan, weekly ads, mobile coupons, pill reminders and more, in addition to the usual text-based product search and store locator functionalities. It was likely that the aisle411 app would eventually get merged into the Walgreens app for a more compelling value proposition for store visitors.

## ONE STARTUP AT A TIME

Location-based services could be deployed in two ways. The first, with a chip placed in each handset, used the same GPS technology that tracked ships and vehicles for years. The second used intelligence in the wireless network to communicate with cell sites to determine the subscriber's location. Initially, there was a lack of consensus among American wireless operators on which way to proceed and the FCC provided no definitive direction when the U.S. regulatory body mandated that all wireless handsets include some type of locating capabilities so emergency calls would automatically include information about where to dispatch rescue services. Wireless infrastructure makers, such as Ericsson, were increasingly looking to the latter solution based on location-finding radio triangulation systems. The network-based locating methods involved triangulating the radio emission of the mobile phone or made use of radio fingerprinting to identify the most likely position of the radiating source.

These local positioning services employed a software process that used the geo-physical location of the mobile unit as part of the algorithm for generating the presentation content. Such location services, however, wouldn't come without the rigors of significant technology innovations. To start with, while such systems could locate a user within a particular cell, they did so without pinpoint accuracy and were initially capable of delivering accuracy within fifty meters in a cellular network. In urban areas, where cells were quite small, such location services naturally fell short. In the meantime, specialized chipmakers continued to improve the accuracy and availability of the GPS technology. The new circuitry was also able to gradually trim the GPS power for use in cellular phones. By late 2000s, smartphones had GPS systems on-board, and with location-aware Internet services, they were helping people to get from point A to point B. The GPS-powered applications now helped people to find family, friends, and colleagues, as well as connect them with services in areas of their vicinity.

Then there was location data, which had been available for quite some time, but it was massively underused. Moreover, when location data was used, it was used in a very simple way, and there was a lot more users could do with all the data generated. The up-and-coming smartphone industry began taking advantage of location as an information source and as a way of creating a richer experience, which was one way to overcome the limitations of the smaller screen. A new breed of startups began to frantically work on the technologies that would enable additional services such as location-finding in emergency, location-based push advertising, and location-based service listings. These upstarts offered location-based services in the realm of traffic and weather reports, driving directions, travel and entertainment information, and restaurant recommendations.

Start with Skyhook Wireless which conceived a metro-area positioning system that leveraged Wi-Fi rather than satellites or cellular towers to deliver precise location data. Ted Morgan and Mike Shean, while selling software to Fortune 500 companies across the United States, were constantly on the road, and to check their e-mails, they used to pull up next to buildings, office parks, or apartment complexes and latch on to someone's open Wi-Fi access point. They were stunned by the sheer amount of Wi-Fi signals around. So they founded

Skyhook Wireless in 2003 to develop the Wi-Fi positioning system (WPS) by taking advantage of the hundreds of millions of Wi-Fi access points throughout the populated areas, allowing the system to consistently provide accurate location information in urban areas and indoors.

Skyhook Wireless, formerly known as Quarterscope, hired an army of students and retirees to drive the U.S. roads in vans laden with electronic-sniffing equipment. The outcome was a location database for determining geographical location using Wi-Fi as the underlying reference system. The Wi-Fi positioning system could determine the location of a mobile device within 10 to 20 meters and could also integrate GPS-enabled devices to provide hybrid positioning. A major breakthrough knocked on the Boston–based company's door in January 2008 when Steve Jobs announced at the Macworld Conference & Expo that the iPhone and the iPod touch would use its Wi-Fi positioning system as the location engine for Google Maps and other apps.

Wi-Fi being an in-building technology worked very well in indoor and urban environments, but Wi-Fi didn't prove effective outside populated areas. Conversely, GPS worked very well in outdoors with a clear view of the sky as per its original design and faced obstructions in indoors where people spent most of their time. Global positioning system remained spotty when it came to the indoors, so the next logical navigation frontier was indoors, where GPS didn't work and maps were often nonexistent. Take Google, who had been expanding its mapping technologies to the point where its Street View technology would become nearly ubiquitous. However, most of Google's indoor navigation was limited to public buildings like airports, malls, train stations, sports stadiums, and museums. So, Apple, who had been working to improve its outdoor mapping capabilities, was getting into indoor navigation as well.

In 2013, Apple acquired WiFiSlam, an indoor navigation startup which enabled a smartphone to pinpoint its location in real-time with up to 2.5 meters of accuracy using just Wi-Fi signal nearby. The two-year-old startup had developed ways for mobile apps to detect a phone user's location in a building for providing step-by-step indoor navigation to retail customer apps and proximity-based social networking. WiFiSlam combined the fingerprint of Wi-Fi networks with information taken from a smartphone via compass and accelerometer. The technology analyzed the signal strengths and unique IDs of all the Wi-Fi networks around it and matched them against a reference data set for the area, either accessed over the Internet or stored on the device. The estimate of location could be sharpened if a gadget moved slightly because WiFiSlam's algorithms could gather multiple fingerprints. Compass data and accelerometer signals capturing a person's footsteps were also used to refine the accuracy of subsequent location fixes as a person moved around.

The other critical aspect in the contrasting worlds of GPS and Wi-Fi was speed and consequently accuracy. While the GPS technology was designed to be slow to be able to effectively figure out the location within a large footprint, it also provided better accuracy: it could get down to about 10 meters. Wi-Fi, on the other hand, worked faster but wasn't as accurate as GPS, getting down to about 20 meters. According to the findings from Yelp, based on its geo-location data, GPS was twice as accurate as Wi-Fi.

However, when these two landmark technologies were put together, the technology overlay of the two worked better than either one performing on its own. The smartphone became the springboard of this powerful mix of GPS tracking and Wi-Fi triangulation to determine an ultra-precise location, possibly within a few centimeters, both for indoors and outdoors. Take Wi-Fi equipment maker Ruckus Wireless, for instance, which integrated a GPS receiver in its outdoor access points to streamline how Wi-Fi network operators determine users' locations. That way the software for its indoor equipment would determine user locations to within six feet.

Companies that developed Wi-Fi networks also had a new pitch for retailers and marketers: use the technology to keep tabs on customers. Places like stores, malls, and airports had started installing Wi-Fi networks to please smartphone-toting users, who used them to get faster Internet access and avoid cellular-data charges. In return, Wi-Fi technology let the network operator keep tabs on what users were doing—from where they were standing to what websites they were visiting. For instance, retailers could learn in what aisle shoppers were most likely to point their smartphone browser to Amazon.com. That way, mall owners had a new means to judge which storefronts attracted the most foot traffic. Moreover, owners of Wi-Fi networks could turn their antennas into virtual billboards, charging a premium for ads sent to users' phones in prime locations.

All such innovations in the Wi-Fi space led to new business opportunities for upstarts. Boingo, one of the biggest operators of Wi-Fi networks in the United States, aimed for a system that tracked traffic patterns in malls and stores by using the signals emitted by shoppers' smartphones as they hunted for Wi-Fi networks. The system would allow retailers and shopping-mall operators to monitor shoppers' locations even when the shoppers weren't logged onto the network. That's possible because Wi-Fi-enabled devices regularly check for available networks by sending signals to surrounding base stations. Then there was Wifarer which aimed to build a software-based indoor positioning technology by taking a venue's pre-existing Wi-Fi setting, create radio-frequency fingerprints, capture these fingerprints, and infer users' locations.

Another exciting prospect was heat-mapping technology which allowed organizations with big Wi-Fi networks to identify customer locations and traffic patterns. The technology worked by triangulating phone signals received by different Wi-Fi base stations. Menlo Park, California–based Nearbuy Systems aimed to sell retailers the technology which cross-referenced the websites shoppers visited on their phones with their physical location in the store. The company offered software that let retailers track which websites a shopper visited when using a store's Wi-Fi network and then overlay that information with data showing where the shopper was in the store. The resulting "heat maps" could show which products were most vulnerable to being tried out in the store but ultimately bought for less online. A department store that learned many of its customers logged on to Amazon.com while in the electronics department, for instance, could move an additional store employee to that area.

It was the sheer density of sensors—receiving signals from global navigation satellites, cell-phone towers, and Wi-Fi hot spots as well as input from gyroscopes, accelerometers, step counters, and altimeters—that processed information to make the "ubiquitous navigation" dream come true. Then there was this integration of new kinds of location data which opened up the possibility of navigating indoors, where GPS signals were weak or nonexistent. The advancements like the ones outlined in this section would continue to help location services get more refined and thus enable a new kind of m-commerce predicated on the fact that retailers would know the moment a customer walked by their front door or when a customer was looking for a particular product.

## THE UBIQUITOUS SENSOR

The GPS sensor appeared to have become one of the most coveted parts in the smartphone anatomy after the camera. Location data opened the floodgates of innovation and possibility to change the face of the mobile landscape. It was evident by now that location could create amazing opportunities by utilizing data to examine context and thus harness creative and powerful marketing products. But there were challenges, too. If there was one factor that had the potential to railroad the momentum created by location apps, it was concerns regarding user privacy.

The prospects of location-aware technology terrified privacy advocators, who feared that the sensitive location data bytes could be abused by employers, insurers, creditors, or even stalkers. It also troubled civil libertarians who worried that another critical wall was falling between the individual and the probing eyes of the outside world. Although the information wouldn't be available to everyone, it could potentially be sold to advertisers and could be made available to law-enforcement agencies, hackers, lawyers in divorce cases and other civil lawsuits, and to nosy employees of companies that build location-tracking systems. In countries with repressive political systems, location-tracking records could also be made available to secret police forces. The real question was whether a system could be developed that would benefit from the location technology while protecting consumers from constant surveillance of the Big Brother. Well aware that privacy concerns could be a land mine, many of the companies aiming to capitalize on location services now began developing necessary safeguards to protect their subscribers. The purpose of these location services is to be of value to customers, and we are certainly not going to do anything they don't want, they said.

Then, in April 2011, Apple triggered privacy alarms with the news that the iPhone kept a database of a handset's location. The Internet went abuzz when hackers Peter Warden and Aladair Allen stumbled upon the unencrypted file on the iOS 4 platform which stored the location data of iPad and iPhone users for over a year. A few days after this scandal erupted, *The Wall Street Journal* reported that Google's Android also collected location data, and instead of storing it away in a file, the data was sent back to Google servers. An Android phone recorded location data every few seconds and transmitted it back to Google several times an hour. Google also used location data to provide traffic information on Google Maps.

Apple, on the other hand, designed its mobile devices to let ad and analytic companies collect personal data. Apple also collected addresses, ages and genders without permission and inconsistent with its policies. Both Apple and Google collected location data from mobile devices to ensure efficient switching between cellular networks and Wi-Fi hotspots.

By 2013, legislators around the world began conceiving regulations that mandated law enforcement agents a warrant before affixing a GPS tracker to a vehicle or using a cell site simulator to locate someone through mobile device or obtaining geo-location data from third-party service providers. These laws-in-the-making would prohibit private investigators and other private individuals from using a GPS device to surreptitiously track someone's location without their consent. But such legislative efforts stopped short of requiring agents or private individuals to obtain a warrant for GPS devices; they also mostly bypassed the issue of whether warrants should be required to obtain geo-location information collected by service providers from smartphones and car-tracking systems like OnStar.

The location apps obtained data in a variety of ways: some apps took GPS data directly from the user's mobile phone while other apps like Foursquare collected location data from mobile users when they explicitly informed the application that they would like to check-in at a particular place. Foursquare—which owned much of the mindshare built around the second-generation location services—also built on location data gleaned from user-submitted content from social networks such as Facebook and Twitter. By creating addictive games around the app, Foursquare built out a database of places on the backs of gallivanting users, additionally encouraging them to broadcast their whereabouts into other social media channels like Facebook and Twitter, as well as leaving tips for others and creating checklists for themselves.

While apps like Foursquare collected location data through explicit means, another key mechanism, embodied by apps like Instagram, relied on implicit means for revealing location at a specific point in time when mobile users took a specific action such as capturing a photo. Foursquare knew where a mobile user was in exchange for alerting him as to who might be nearby; Instagram knew where a mobile user was in exchange for unlocking rewards or broadcasting that he was at a cool place. One of the biggest draws of Facebook's acquisition of Instagram was the extent of how much access Instagram had to location data that Facebook could now tap. While Instagram did an incredible job innovating around the camera software and social engagement features, it was also able to briefly capture a user's location implicitly at the time an image was captured, so much so that if a mobile user took an Instagram at a sporting event and then clicked on the location-stamp, it was possible to see a kaleidoscope of other Instagrams from the same ballpark.

There had to be a level of transparency where consumers clearly knew when they were sharing their location and with whom. People want the ability to control what offers they receive and when they receive them, whether through opt-in or check-in or preference-type settings. Take the credit card value chain, for instance, in which credit card companies know where their customers purchase items. Likewise, mobile phone operators know their subscribers' location, as do the smartphone manufacturers and those who provide operating systems like Android on these phones. Last but not least, social networks like Facebook and Twitter know the whereabouts of their users as they capture data about them every time they log a status update on the go. For a mobile user, the trade is quite simple: offer your location at a specific point in time, or your patterns, and in exchange for that information, an app will offer you something—a deal, a coupon, or information about who or what is around you.

If the apps made people's lives easier and if they offered game-like fun to get users hooked, they would appeal to mobile users at large. It's quite plausible that for the right product experiences, most mobile consumers would be willing to share their location, giving the developers of location applications a goldmine of data to explore. Once the application developers uncovered robust business models, these apps could be incredibly valuable to businesses large and small who wanted to act on this data but didn't want to be seen as grafting it without permission.

The second largest conundrum in the location realm that everybody had been trying to solve was persistent, passive, real-time location which let people know where a certain user was at any given time without check-in information. While Google's Latitude and Apple's Find My Friends apps constantly beamed out where users were to followers, the services hardly made any inroads. Even Foursquare was based on the check-in model; if nobody checked in, nobody showed up. There was a consensus that real-time information was the future of location and that it was just a matter of time before someone cracked this piece of the puzzle.

There were applications like EchoEcho, for instance, which instead of focusing on check-ins and deals, simply made it easy for mobile users to find out where their friends were and let them set up a meeting. And EchoEcho provided this functionality with just a few taps. To ensure privacy, the smartphone user's location was automatically shared with the friends he tried to locate. From there, the user could either use the built-in chat function to organize a meeting or use the app's built-in location database to decide on which coffee shop, restaurant or other public place he wanted to meet at. Users who didn't have the app installed would receive a text message and could then use the service's web app to update their location.

There were some other apps—like Highlight and Glympse—that worked passively to collect location data. Glympse arrived at a time when its competitors were the original, location-based social networks such as Loopt and Brightkite—all gone by 2012. The location-sharing app, which debuted back in 2009, believed there was value in the more utilitarian functionality of sharing location with friends on a more individualized basis. Instead of offering a social network for check-ins or making location continually public through a social network, Glympse would automatically share mobile user's current location for a set amount of time, allowing friends or colleagues to track his approach as he headed his way for an event or a meeting.

With Glympse Groups, for instance, the idea was to allow a group of users to share their location during common activities, like sporting events, conferences, meetings, or social gatherings. Glympse's calendar integration allowed users to automatically send out location updates associated with a particular event, so participants could avoid the "on my way" and "running late" e-mails, calls and texts. All these apps worked in the background to grab location, whether or not mobile users were actively using that application. Such apps were useful in helping people locate items, find their friends, or track their children, but their intrusiveness also made people feel uneasy. Higher battery degradation was another crucial roadblock for these apps.

## APP BECOMES PLATFORM

A key issue hinged on how location services sucked the energy marrow out of a mobile phone's battery. The location-tracking apps drained smartphone batteries by constantly running GPS in the background or pinging cellular towers. If app developers could reliably add location features that were light on the battery and were secure and private, the industry might see the dawn of the age of persistent location sooner than later. The mobile phone industry considered a variety of solutions, including replacing Wi-Fi with Bluetooth as a means of wireless communications. The integration of Bluetooth gear into Wi-Fi routers would not only extend battery life but also boost the indoor efficiency by 5 to 10 feet.

But the most practical solution came from Geoloqi, a Portland, Oregon–based company which pioneered the idea of geo-fencing by allowing events to trigger as users passed by a certain location. When a person was nowhere near a geo-fence, the mobile device wouldn't ping data servers constantly and that would ramp down GPS to conserve battery life. Moreover, the size of the data signal connecting phone to the back-end server could be made smaller in terms of packet length and thus further reduce the battery life drain.

The idea behind geo-fencing was to target consumers when they were nearby and target them in a way that the promotions got hyper-local, like beaming a promotion for umbrellas to people within a ten-mile radius during a rainstorm. The geo-fencing technology was also seen as an answer to the dreaded problem of showrooming, where a shopper came into a store to see an item but then made the purchase online after finding a better price via smartphone. While consumers figured out how to use smartphones to retailers' disadvantage by checking prices elsewhere, large chain stores fumbled around for a way to use handsets to boost sales. Eventually, large chains and brands began employing geo-fencing through sensors in their stores to offer customized information and virtual coupons delivered through smartphones. The geo-fencing techniques not only promised to speed up the shopping process, they also kept mobile consumers connected to the brand.

Geoloqi—co-founded by Amber Case and Aaron Perecki in 2010—got some early traction with its customizable GPS-based mobile app of the same name that enabled automatic check-ins, location sharing and location-based reminders.

The app let people set reminders, rules and notes based on their geographic location; once the app was downloaded, a user could set SMS notes that were received only when he entered a specific location. What made this app unique wasn't its instant popularity but the fact that soon after the launch the company began to receive calls from developers in the enterprise and government sectors as well as from wireless operators. They wanted to use the platform behind the app to build their own apps. That was an interesting development for Geoloqi managers because it was hard to have a reliable revenue model for an app. An enterprise solution for app developers made much more sense.

The first generation of location services didn't have the entire solution and that left developers either struggling with incomplete systems or they were forced to build out their own location features. Location accuracy, battery life, and location-aware push messaging were hard to build and even harder to implement for app developers. Geoloqi quickly moved in to fill the gap and soon the idea of turning complicated real-time location-aware data into a ready-to-use platform for developers took on a life of its own. The Portland–based company now found itself in the midst of disrupting the first generation of location services. In fact, Geoloqi was bridging the first and second generations of location services by making it easier for developers to merge location services into their apps. In the end, its own app proved more of a showcase to the real work that Geoloqi would eventually be doing behind the scene.

It's important to note that not all developers were aiming for pure location apps; a predominant majority of apps wanted location as a feature. In that case, a company couldn't just hire three or four developers and make them work on something as challenging as battery management, data storage and geo-fencing. Geoloqi provided developers with persistent background location tracking that could incorporate location data from cellular, GPS, and Wi-Fi networks in a way that was battery efficient. Developers could create geo-fencing, automatic check-ins, and location-based messaging, the most promising opportunities for marketers to target consumers. Then there was rich analytics for tracking users, dwell time, visitors, and security. Geoloqi provided all the necessary tools to help bring location services to the mainstream.

Companies like Geoloqi were demonstrating how location-based services were poised to turn a corner. So, suddenly, Geoloqi found itself at the forefront of finding solutions to some of the core issues that hindered the advent of second-generation location services. As mentioned early in this chapter, the holy grail of mobile geo-location services was persistent, real-time data delivery to the mobile device—not an easy feat to pull off. The real world wasn't necessarily all about advertising or wanting to see where friends were; it was also about knowing where something was happening when you needed to know. So the intelligent way Geoloqi handled background location tracking quickly got noticed by companies and government agencies.

Like many of its peers in the location realm, the geo-fencing services pioneer from Portland was eventually acquired by Redlands, California–based map provider Esri in October 2012. Nevertheless, the Geoloqi episode marked a shift from cool apps to tangible infrastructure that aimed to monetize location-based services. Soon there were other players vying for location-based platforms that connected the dots within the world of mobile commerce. Take Zaarly, an optimized mobile Craigslist founded in May 2011. The upstart focused on sales of goods, rather than services, within a given location and required users to verify their identities with an e-mail address, a phone number and a Facebook account. Would-be buyers posted what they wanted and would-be sellers could search offers based on price and distance. The buyers then chose among the responses to their offers, and when a transaction was complete, Zaarly took a cut.

## THE GROUPON EFFECT

Groupon was another important case study in the m-commerce realm. Groupon's early value proposition centered on being a marketing tool to connect consumers and merchants. In 2006, Andrew Mason was music major, getting a graduate degree in public policy at the University of Chicago. On the side, he was doing contract work building databases at a company founded and funded by an entrepreneur named Eric Lefkofsky. In January 2007, with Lefkofsky's backing, Mason started working on a site called ThePoint.com, which helped people work together to accomplish campaigns, including community projects. Mason, the irreverent programmer and musician, eventually turned the failed social action site into the daily deals phenomenon for selling marked-down spa packages and half-off pizzas in 2008.

Over the years, a number of Silicon Valley startups had tried many forms of deal sites, but Groupon was the first to really make it work, and did so fiercely. The formula was simple and compelling. People were sent e-mails of offers for, say, a local restaurant. If they bought it, they got a bargain, Groupon got a commission and the restaurant won new patrons. With somewhere in the neighborhood of 100,000,000 subscribers on its e-mail list, Groupon could drive feet through the doors like crazy. Then there came the Groupon prosperity when *Forbes* magazine called it the "Fastest Growing Company Ever." Daily deal services took off because they seemed to offer something for everyone: small businesses got a novel way to bring new customers in the door, shoppers got a discount, and the deal providers got a cut of every sale.

Mason's goal was to make Groupon the Amazon.com of local commerce and the mantra at the online-coupon company was that it was going to build the operating system for local commerce. Local commerce was a multi-trillion dollar business and Groupon set its sights on this large but mostly disorganized ecosystem that connected merchants with consumers. In just two years' time, the company ballooned from 37 employees to 9,625 staff members and from serving five markets in the United States to 175 in North America alone. And then there was massive expansion abroad. The vision of the "platform of local commerce" was so grand that Groupon walked away from Google's US$6 billion offer in November 2010. Groupon went public in just three years, earning a valuation of US$16.5 billion and delivering the biggest tech IPO since Google.

Small businesses were excited at first about this new way to attract customers in a post-Yellow Pages world, but soon they found out that customers who bought deals overwhelmed the businesses, spent the bare minimum, and never returned. Eventually, the deal fatigue raised questions about whether Groupon and its competitors could continue their hyper-growth. Groupon did create a new market but it now faced plenty of challengers such as Google-backed LivingSocial. The daily-deals space was looking a bit overfished. As a result of that, Groupon found itself searching for alternative ways to make money, like buying movie tickets, watches and other goods, and selling them to shoppers. Groupon expanded into many new segments, from selling lower-priced and simpler deals on restaurants and spas to more complex and pricey arenas, including travel, physical goods and luxury items.

The Chicago–based local discounts service began shifting steadily toward deals that stayed valid for longer. By 2012, Groupon was essentially in two businesses: the original daily-deals business which had evolved into what was more or less a marketing platform for local businesses and Groupon Goods which was a selection of products for sale, usually at an attractive discount. Groupon Goods—which the company called curated e-commerce—had been performing far better than the local-deals business. Now Groupon didn't see itself as a mere coupon service, but a discovery engine, which helped people find out new places, for instance, where to get their fingernails painted, and as a result, the discovered merchant benefited. The daily deals behemoth expanded into restaurant and retail segments, and positioned itself as the linchpin of the operating system of local commerce.

However, to fulfill that grand vision, Groupon needed to deliver an end-to-end commerce solution for local merchants—from marketing to scheduling to integration with POS systems—to offer tracking, analytics, and better ways for merchants to retain customers while finding new ones. For that, it would have to move upstream and serve as the entry point for local transactions. For a start, Groupon launched an iPad-based point-of-sale service for restaurants across the United States. The service, called Breadcrumb, was in essence a replacement of a cash register and had been tested in some hundred New York restaurants, bars, and cafes before the launch. With Breadcrumb, Groupon began to look less like a LivingSocial competitor and more like a Square or PayPal rival. To fulfill its dream of becoming the operating system of local commerce, Groupon needed to put an iPad at the front door of every restaurant; teach them about loyalty programs; teach them about customer relationships; and teach them about follow-up and frequency of communication.

The Chicago–based deals site initially missed the mobile beat and soon found perception of the company changing from the fastest-growing e-commerce outfit ever to one that couldn't keep control of that runaway growth. So, to execute this expansion and transform its outdated, non-mobile business model, Groupon acquired more than a dozen companies within a short span of time. Groupon was now in the process of trying to transform from a growth company with a narrow focus on daily deals into a mature firm with a multi-faceted business. However, the growth was hardly organic and

Groupon mostly bought copycat companies to expand into new areas. Because it was buying up companies, rather than scaling out its own technology, Groupon was basically running on dozens of incompatible platforms. The logic that Groupon was more of a sales business than a technology company wasn't much helpful either.

Groupon, who now saw its future in mobile commerce, wanted to push deals to people when they were on the move and near a point of purchase. Its acquisition of Kima Labs was a clear sign of how the new e-commerce darling was looking to mobile for future growth. Kima Labs, founded by Amazon veterans Blake Scholl and Jason Crawford, focused on mobile shopping through the mobile barcode reading app Barcode Hero and mobile payment app TapBuy. Like Groupon, TapBuy offered daily deals and processed transactions using credit card information provided by users while grouping purchases together and adding coupons to purchases. It would be worthwhile to mention that the news of Kima Labs' acquisition broke just hours after Groupon announced it would buy Hyperpublic, a New York City–based upstart which had spent a couple of years developing geo-location technology and putting deals and events on top of it.

But Groupon's most crucial acquisition was probably Ditto. me, a mobile-first company that carried the conviction that location was the first piece of a larger, contextualized world. The Ditto app discreetly incorporated a user's intent into the equation which was something very different from Groupon's larger mobile blueprint. The acquisition marked Groupon's bid to transform itself from a glorified coupon distribution service to a mobile powerhouse that aimed to drive foot traffic to stores in real-time. Proximity was one of the crucial elements in real-world location but just because something was close didn't mean it was useful too. Unrelated and out of context coupons were apparently of no value. Ditto.me added a layer of context on top of location so that real-time, context-based coupons could actually bring value to a business on its own terms. A smartphone user would use Ditto to look for recommended locations, pick the type of food, and organize the group to meet there from within the app. A user, for instance, picked a type of restaurant or a movie, picked her friends, and let the restaurants or movie theatres bid on the business.

The inception of Geoloqi, Groupon, and other upstarts covered in this chapter was a testament that location was for real, and that it was going to radically alter the shape of the m-commerce landscape. This chapter provided a detailed treatment of location-based services and established how they fit into the larger m-commerce setup. The next chapter takes a more focused look at Foursquare as the poster child of location services which evolved and ultimately merged with context phenomenon and social networks to give birth to the idea of social discovery. This class act at the crossroads of mobile and computing industries is chronicled to further explore the anatomy of the location-based commerce nirvana.

# **7** THE BIRTH OF A LOCATION PLATFORM

*"Let's make cities easier to use."*

— Dennis Crowley, co-founder and chief
executive officer, Foursquare

When Dennis Crowley headed to New York in the year 2000 after earning a bachelor's degree in communications from Syracuse University, he thought he would end up in magazine journalism. Instead, he made it to Vindigo, a maker of city guides for Palm Pilot personal digital assistants (PDAs). That's where Crowley envisaged the idea of city discovery with a social twist; he even tried to get Vindigo managers on-board, but they were too busy creating rich content for the PDA which was then considered the gadget of the future. The term smartphone had just emerged in the tech world and the vision of social media was still years away.

In 2001, Vindigo went through a series of layoffs and Crowley was let go. He spent the summer trying to line up interviews, but jobs were scarce, so eventually he enrolled at New York University's Interactive Telecommunications Program. There he met user interface designer Alex Rainert with whom Crowley shared interests in gaming, mobile, social, music, and sports. Crowley shared with Rainert the idea of check-in using text message in a social network setting and the two started working on a prototype for a class project. The work subsequently became their thesis, and after their graduation in 2003, Crowley and Rainert turned it into a startup venture with the name Dodgeball. The upstart aimed to connect mobile phone users in a Friendster-like way by using text messages instead of a web browser. Mobile phone users could "check in" at bars or restaurants by sending a text, and all of their "friends" on the service would get a text within the location. Mobile users would get points for checking in.

But smartphones were still in their infancy and the social media landscape was nowhere to be seen. Venture capitalists were obviously reluctant to extend any support for a simple text-based service, so after Dodgeball gathered some initial momentum, it was sold to Google in 2005. It was the same year when Google made the landmark acquisition of Android. The web search giant was probably in a very early stage of sorting out its mobile roadmap and Dodgeball proved a small fry in the bigger scheme of things. Whether it was shallow user adoption or internal power struggles, the Dodgeball founders lost interest in the project and left Google after two years. The project essentially went nowhere and eventually Google shut down the service on January 14, 2009. That's when Crowley saw an opportunity to revive his long-held dream of a location-based social network. The advent of the iPhone had unleashed a whole new market for what Crowley had originally wanted to create with Dodgeball.

By then he had already joined hands with Naveen Selvadurai, a programmer whom he had come to know in the burgeoning New York tech scene. After leaving Google, Crowley found work at a New York company called Area/Code where Selvadurai had a desk around the corner from Crowley. Selvadurai was the expert on the iPhone. They had been sketching the blue-print of the new service for a year while hanging out at Think Coffee in New York's East Village. Eventually, when Google closed the door on Dodgeball, they started coding for the new social network with the intention of finishing it in time for the South By Southwest (SXSW) interactive show in March 2009. Foursquare was born from the ashes of Dodgeball and launched at the 2009 SXSW show. It was the same event where Twitter famously seized the moment and ultimately propelled itself into a multi-billion dollar company.

Foursquare—a geographical location-based social net-work—allowed mobile users to share their location with friends by checking in via a smartphone app or through a text message. It was part city guide and part mobile friend finder. Foursquare quickly became the darling of the new media. The location-centric social app constantly scanned mobile users to see if they were near friends or places they usually liked to visit. The service used GPS signals to allow mobile users to "check in" at places so they could meet new people, invite friends to join up and leave tips for others who would check in later. But unlike early GPS applications that were always-on and made phones seem like tracking devices from a spy movie, Foursquare revealed users' location when they specifically told the app to do so and only to a select group of people they chose. To make it fun, Foursquare introduced a basic form of game mechanics that appealed to distinct groups of users and was critical to this location-based social network's early success in user engagement and retention.

In the early going, when Foursquare users didn't have many friends to interact with, the app allowed users to collect digital "badges" for accomplishments like checking out new places or events and thus kept users engaged on their own. A user who checked in at a venue the most of times could become the "mayor" of the venue, claim territory, and allow merchants to establish loyalty. Mayorships also encouraged friendless users on Foursquare to engage with strangers. And by the time people got bored with badges and mayorships, they had already formed a social network on Foursquare and the utility of knowing friends' location became a big draw for them. It was this intersection of mobility and social networks that lifted Foursquare to rock stardom in an ever evolving media landscape.

The promise of social networking was converging with the smart portable search. Points were awarded for checking in at various venues and users could connect their Foursquare accounts to their Facebook and Twitter accounts, leading to an update when a check-in was registered. Foursquare was also unique in the sense that it was a social tool outside the desktop world and fully relied on the power of mobility. By December 2009, Foursquare had spread to hundred cities across the world. However, the problem was that Foursquare was mostly seen as a cool app for rich kids. It was true in the sense that it mostly catered to people in large cities and night-life types bouncing from one spot to another. Foursquare, rather than innovating on the confluence of time and space, was seen as being too much about places.

Over four years, Foursquare had logged over 3 billion check-ins from its 30 million users, providing the company with an astounding collection of location data which it in turn made available to other apps. However, check-ins, the cor-nerstone of Foursquare's early growth and its main source of data points, were no longer what they used to be. In 2010, Foursquare was noticing more people were using Foursquare but not checking in. Foursquare, which had grown from two guys working out of Think Coffee to a local "check-in" service, had come a long way since its inception at the SXWX show in 2009. Another challenge for Crowley was how to take this Dodgeball replacement to mainstream.

Moreover, by late 2010, Foursquare wasn't the only cool kid on the location block; a new wave of startups was out there to draw on smartphone location data and deliver a range of social, commercial and information services. And these mobile apps in the social location space were increasingly getting traction. To make this all even more competitive, social behe-moths like Facebook and Twitter, which Foursquare seam-lessly used to score check-ins and accomplishments, were turning themselves into one-stop shops by adding games and utilities while building the entire business on their social platforms. But the fact that mobile users were more likely to go out and join activities rather than just spend hours in front of a desktop gave Foursquare a crucial edge. Furthermore,

Foursquare knew a lot more about its users and that gave it a powerful tool in social monetization.

## SOCIAL DISCOVERY

Dennis Crowley had once compared Foursquare's check-ins to Google's web crawlers scanning the Internet for new websites. Foursquare had come a long way over the years, but it was still mostly about check-ins. The problem was that check-ins were a nice tool for adding depth to more interesting activities, like photo sharing, but they were an afterthought and were not an app-worthy activity in their own right. Moreover, that way, Foursquare had been better at helping its users find ways to spend their money than at making any money of its own. So Foursquare decided to finally de-emphasize check-in and the game it had created around becoming "mayor" of a location. That led to the company's evolution from an app that was primarily focused around helping people to find their friends to finding out more about the world that they lived in. It was inevitably going to be a massive shift from being a simple check-in service to becoming a recommendation and search utility.

In summer 2012, amid a hypercompetitive environment, Foursquare, instead of congratulating itself on achieving darling status and a crazy valuation, disassembled the entire app and put it back together again. The new Foursquare was a discovery engine, a deals vehicle, and a sharing machine all rolled into one; check-in was now just one piece of its functionality. The redesign capitalized on three years that Foursquare had spent in collecting data on the way users interacted with the app. The Explore tab now populated suggestions based on time of day, relevancy, location, and tips and habits of friends and strangers, all without requiring a search. The location aspect of the app got a new shine with a snappier map interface that let users see where their friends were in real-time. In the map view, Explore showed friends who had checked in nearby with icons of their faces, as well as icons of recommended venues in that vicinity.

The Foursquare DNA wouldn't change with the new version; but the focus would shift to the Explore button which gave users suggestions on where to go, based on information like the popularity of nearby places and past check-ins. It was still incredibly important for Foursquare to keep people checking in because that was a starting point for so much of the data that powered Explore. Foursquare understood this and thus simplified the check-in process by moving the check-in button to the top right and speeding up the process on the back-end. Check-in was also crucial in the Foursquare scheme of things because it provided the location dynamo with a distribution network apart from rich data. The truth was that with 2 billion check-ins Foursquare was now putting that mountain of data to work by pushing out smarter recommendations and highlighting more ways for people to find new places. The new Foursquare, however, de-emphasized the points, relying less on game mechanics to motivate people and focusing more on providing useful recommendations.

The local mobile paradigm had evolved from a simple check-in service to a robust recommendation engine. So Foursquare redesigned the app to emphasize local search and recommendations over check-ins as a way to get users to choose Foursquare instead of alternatives. When someone searched with Foursquare by typing in a keyword or asking what was interesting, Foursquare put a promotion. The activity around places included check-ins, likes on venues, tips that people left, the people who liked the tips left by people, people saving things to their list, and sending those to other people. So it wasn't really about the decline of the check-in but the emergence of search and discovery. In fact, the check-in data allowed Foursquare to make great recommendations. Foursquare still got around 5 million check-ins per day as of 2013, and the influx of check-ins was something that the company could rely on. Foursquare was constantly getting signal of what's interesting and not interesting through the massive check-in data.

Foursquare now steadily began adding features like restaurant recommendations and passive location direction based on app user's prior experiences. It was no longer just about finding where friends were, but discovering where people should go. Foursquare also began to offer deals, menus and special hours. Next up, it provided the ability for users to add personal bios of 160-character or less either on its website or users could import their bios directly from their Twitter accounts. That way, people could start following other Foursquare users that they didn't necessarily know but with whom they shared common interests. That marked another milestone for the social discovery phenomenon as it notified users when they were near someone unfamiliar but whom they might find interesting. The social discovery concept served as the natural extension of social networking by focusing on introducing users to new people.

Foursquare was able to reinvent its product and the location space at large by rolling out new features at the precise moment when its user base primed. The company was steadily moving toward providing better discovery tools for consumers and better loyalty and efficiency tools for merchants. But instead of employing a massive sales force and entering the daily deals and coupon race, like what Groupon did, Foursquare chose to leverage its passionate user community and pioneer a new form of rewards-based advertising platform. Next in line for Foursquare was the possibility of an expanded payment role where it could close the loop on redemptions, helping people to discover a place, get a cut for facilitating the customer visit, and complete the transaction. Merchants could also benefit through Foursquare-enabled NFC tags that encouraged mobile users to check in and see special offers, opening up a new channel of communication between the business and the consumer.

However, plenty of competition—from Groupon to Social Passport to Yelp—was awaiting Foursquare here. The local advertising and deals market had heated up as Facebook, Google, Twitter, Yelp, and even Groupon had started to focus more heavily on location-based offerings. Foursquare had been slow in ramping up its advertising products; now the redesign and early ad product called "promoted updates" placed Foursquare much more squarely in competition with those big names, making it all the more crucial that the company hit its mark. Foursquare was becoming more of a personalized local search engine that could walk people into local stores and restaurants. And Foursquare's early competitors—including Loopt, Gowalla, Whrrl, Brightkite and Hot

Potato—had all disappeared, either folding their businesses or shutting after being acquired.

The biggest question mark for these upstarts was how to make money. People were still warming to the idea of location sharing when Foursquare upgraded its app to offer personalized coupons and made an audacious bid to make money through its location-based social network. Earlier, Foursquare offered specials for users, but it didn't charge merchants for special billing of those coupons. Now, when users discovered new places and businesses in Foursquare's Explore feature, merchants would get a chance to highlight their offers to users. Foursquare would charge US$10 for allowing merchants to pay for special placement of personalized local offers. The local discovery icon apparently wanted to make money by getting better at connecting people with places. Ultimately, the real value didn't just come through helping consumers find shops, but also by helping merchants find their customers.

Foursquare began rolling out promoted updates and promoted specials with a handful of large chains, including Gap, Old Navy, Hilton, JC Penney, Best Buy and Walgreens, as well as some smaller merchants. The "action rate" for the ads was about 3 percent, with more than 50 percent of users who engaged with a promoted update checking into the merchant's location within 72 hours. Interestingly, a lot of people didn't see promoted update as paid advertising because it was not an ad-sponsored story or banner advertisement. That made Foursquare one of the few social networks with purchasing intent, which meant monetization could be non-annoying and high revenue per thousand (RPM).

During its first three years, Foursquare shunned traditional advertising in favor of creating a fun and increasingly powerful product that worked for both consumers and merchants. While the upstart from New York made a small amount of money on things like brand promotions and allowing merchants to claim their Foursquare venue page online, it really hadn't had a reliable monetization engine. Now, with the promoted updates, it was leveraging its Explore technology to match promoted updates to the people most likely to act on them. When users clicked on the Explore tab on their Foursquare mobile app, they saw promoted updates from nearby businesses that wanted to prompt some kind of action from them. Businesses who bought promoted updates would pay on a cost-per-action basis, which could be anything from a user visiting a venue page or unlocking a special deal to checking in a store or loading a product discount coupon.

A little after the redesign launch, Foursquare announced a new feature for merchants as well: local updates. The launch of its first major monetization product, promoted updates, discount offers and other targeted messages served up to mobile users via the app's local discovery engine, Explore. Now Foursquare opened up this new channel to allow merchants to communicate with their customers and lead them into their stores. Merchants could send out updates like daily specials and events, complete with text, photos, and deals from their Foursquare dashboard. If a Foursquare user checked into a business several times or "liked" it on the app, she would start receiving that business' updates when her phone location indicated she was in the same area.

The "local updates" feature was made to be used by small independent merchants and large chains alike. Large chains were given the option of either issuing updates across their entire fleet of storefronts or to individual locations. The launch showed how all pieces of Foursquare's business plan were coming together into a potential money maker. Local updates clearly demonstrated how Foursquare could bring value to merchants with its 20 million plus users and a lot of rich data. It was also a crucial product for Foursquare because its ultimate goal was to create a robust mobile advertising product and thus to be able to charge merchants for the full suite of tools. Foursquare enjoyed an advantage because it was built as a mobile-first company and it understood how to craft mobile advertisements that worked for its audience.

Foursquare was getting its act together and starting to make use of all of its big data. With its more than 2.5 billion check-ins and even more useful behavior data, it was learning a lot about how to bring users together with interesting places. As Foursquare learned to harvest more and more data and turn it into tailored recommendations, it became more of a person-alized mobile local search engine for its 25 million users. Since it not only understood what was near a person but what was relevant to him based on his tastes, his friends' tastes, the time of day and other signals, Foursquare was able to generate better results than a traditional search engine. There was an opportunity for Foursquare to start scooping up local search advertising revenue if it could make its Explore engine a go-to search and discovery resource for more people. The mobile Internet's premier location service claimed that 20 percent of people who searched for a place in Foursquare ended up checking-in at the location within three days.

# FOURSQUARE AT CROSSROADS

There were a ton of companies coming at the idea of charting user location via mobile, and what to do with it once they acquired that information, including Yelp, Google, Facebook, Groupon, Square, Instagram and more. Foursquare was now being perceived as a one-trick pony and pundits reckoned that check-in could become to Foursquare what the GPS was to TomTom when satellite navigation went into phones. The risk for Foursquare especially became stark when similar check-in features were built into Facebook, Yelp, Google, and Trip Advisor. Especially, Yelp, which had a market cap of US$1.2 billion in 2012, boasted 84 million unique monthly visitors, including 8.2 million visitors from mobile devices. Foursquare's time to do recommendations and couponing was before Yelp established critical mass and copied the playful game, matching Foursquare Mayors with its very own Dukes.

But when Foursquare deemphasized the check-in game and moved to local recommendations and couponing, it also pushed ads to those mobile users who still came to play the check-in game. Foursquare also made maps special; it took maps that were blank and put dots on them to help mobile users figure out what to do. Foursquare—now largely a food recommendations machine—was challenging Yelp as the de facto place to answer "what should I grab to eat?" What was once a cool way to see where your friends were evolved into one of the most important sources of data on where urbanites liked to eat and drink.

However, according to some critics, Foursquare was stuck in a twilight zone where it was neither search nor social. If it wanted to compete with search, Foursquare would have to contend with Google, Facebook, and Yelp. On the other hand, If Foursquare wanted to compete in couponing, it would line up against Groupon, LivingSocial and other cash-rich companies with many more users. Competition was abounding in the coming-of-age location business. Apple had launched Find My Friends on its iOS 5 platform while Google had introduced the Latitude app back in 2009. There were also dozens of location-sharing apps and services like Life360 and Location Labs which targeted at families, businesses and other communities. Evidently, Foursquare was to compete in a crowded market against better-funded competitors with bigger established user bases. Take Facebook and its robust location service "Nearby" as a case study.

Facebook's first "Foursquare-killer" was a pretty bare bones way to check-in to a spot and tag who mobile user was hanging out with; Places failed because people didn't manually check-in enough at locations. After Places flopped, Facebook snatched up Gowalla, a Foursquare competitor co-founded in 2007 by Josh Williams and Scott Raymond. The social media behemoth also bought Glancee, an app that emerged out of 2012's obsession with ambient location services. Foursquare's chief competitor Gowalla had apparently gone to Facebook to challenge Foursquare's dominance in social location. But where did Glancee come in? Glancee was all about ambient social geo-data and it removed the need to check-in. Another benefit was that Glancee mined Facebook for interest data, which was then used to make social connections. Facebook just home-brewed its own Foursquare as a result of these twin acquisitions.

Facebook was leaping into the local discovery and search market with an upgrade to its mobile Nearby feature, which would allow users to find relevant places based on social signals and other data. Nearby, which initially used to only display friend check-ins, would now offer a lot more data on local places, including ratings, recommendations and business information. Facebook users could see a list of places that Facebook believed were relevant to them based on friend check-in data, likes and user recommendations. They could browse different categories and subcategories or search for specific businesses. Individual business listings told mobile users which of their friends liked that business and other pertinent information like address, distance and hours. Facebook was also providing user ratings for businesses.

Facebook's new mobile location product had social discovery as a primary focus. Nearby helped mobile users discover nightlife, shopping, restaurants and more based on the Likes, check-ins, and recommendations of their friends and other users. There were detailed sub-categories so mobile users could browse for restaurants, sports bars, or shopping spots such as clothing, electronics, groceries, or books. Results shown on a split-screen map and list gave mobile users a plenty of context from listings showing a business' name, category, profile picture, address, distance, star rating, and the names of friends who Like it. People were already spending so much time on Facebook that they might be happy to stay on it to find local businesses rather than opening another app. Moreover, people wanted recommendations they could trust, the ones that came from people they knew who shared their tastes—their friends—not from strangers. Nearby let mobile users discover the world through their friends' eyes.

Local discovery services worked if accompanied by plenty of data. While Foursquare had around 30 million users, Facebook's location services had 250 million users a month. Facebook's plentiful data provided accurate suggestions of what to check out. With Nearby evolving into Facebook's own Foursquare, brands would have a direct line to the 600 million people who logged into Facebook on mobile. And this was just the beginning—the feature would grow as users started checking in, rating and reviewing local businesses. Nearby also provided a crystal ball of how serious Facebook was in mobile and location-based services.

With an update to a quaint little "Nearby" tab, Facebook's ambitious mobile strategy was finally taking shape. The company was back in the mobile check-in sphere and this time it was way better prepared. Nearby was a truly mobile-first interface designed for browsing over typing that worked based on a relevancy-ranking algorithm. The tracking feature would run in the background on smartphones whether or not the user was actively engaging with the app. So Facebook could eventually use that location data to tailor ads to customers based on their current whereabouts as well as their personal preferences. Evidently, if Nearby gained traction, it could mean big things for Facebook's mobile revenue stream. Nearby could help Facebook become more useful to mobile users, who were very intent driven when they searched for things. That, in turn, could help Facebook tap into the local advertising market.

Nearby would pit Facebook against Yelp, Foursquare, and Google. Foursquare and Yelp offered rich content; moreover, mobile users were trained to navigate through their services. If local businesses took their proverbial business to Facebook, Yelp's ad-powered revenue stream could be seriously endangered. But the local-reviews leader hedged its bets against Facebook considerably better than Foursquare did. Yelp was stuffed to the gills with unique, user-submitted data. On the other hand, Facebook's aggressive new mobile direction was materializing with standard check-in feature and that brought an existential threat to Foursquare's social experience. When Facebook—with its 600 million mobile users—would enable local search, could it be the last nail in Foursquare's coffin?

Industry observers increasingly asked if Foursquare would become the next highly-funded casualty in the social media sphere? There were other factors too that made Foursquare vulnerable. For instance, most of Foursquare's members used it to complement a major social network, either Facebook or Twitter. Second, Foursquare had a big goal of creating an ambient-aware location service that would recommend people, places and events happening nearby, but the hardware wasn't quite up to snuff yet. In the meantime, Foursquare was using location data to take on Yelp and Google. Third, the ever-changing buttons of the Foursquare app were a testament that the data science behind its recommendations and push notifications could be an extremely tricky business.

As chronicled above, Facebook, Google, Yelp, Instagram, Groupon, Twitter and dozens of other popular apps offered location-enabled features. They had moved beyond the "check-in" concept, which in any case never really caught on with mobile users, and began offering location-based notifications and location-aware services. Foursquare was stuck in social media no man's land; it simply couldn't afford to follow industry leaders instead of becoming a leader itself.

# A WIKIPEDIA FOR PLACES

Foursquare was positioning itself as a location platform, but location was a moving target, and Foursquare confronted an inflection point where more people were using the app but not checking in.As location features crept into every corner of the social experience, checking-in didn't provide the buzz that it used to. However, the huge amount of data Foursquare had collected over the course of its existence was feeding the huge demand from social apps. As a result, Foursquare was undergoing a transformation of sorts, again, from a mobile location-reporting and recommendation tool to the social web's key supplier of place data. Foursquare's shift from an app to a bona fide platform came just in time. The location-based social network was now becoming the Wikipedia for places. It was a classic example of data crowd sourcing.

By 2012, Foursquare's 25 million active users had generated more than 2.5 billion check-ins in a period of almost four years. However, Foursquare wasn't entirely dependent on just its users anymore for a lot of its data. Thanks to the Foursquare API, the company got location data from lots of different apps. Foursquare had become a powerhouse data provider to the mobile Internet at large—a sort of utility service for geographical information. Any app developer could pull from this vast collection of places database. For instance, Instagram's location-tagging service was powered by Foursquare. Every Instagram picture that had a location attached to it sent a data signal to Foursquare about that place of interest. Other companies with a much bigger pool of resources—Facebook and Google—also provided geodata to developers, but Foursquare had done a superior job of keeping its crowd-sourced data fresh.

A number of companies relied on Foursquare's map data and what developers could potentially do with that. Any app that did anything with location was generally polling from Foursquare's location data. Foursquare's database had more than 50 million places of interest in it, and it changed frequently. When a mobile user shot a video in Vine, scribbled a reminder in Evernote, made a post on Path, or snapped a photo in Instagram, he could see a little banner pop-up that said "Powered by Foursquare." By way of its API, used by some 40,000 developers in 2012, Foursquare powered location search in a wide range of third-party apps, including Evernote, Uber, Flickr and Jawbone. The relationship between Foursquare and its API partners was mutually beneficial: Foursquare had one of the best map data sets out there and made it available. In exchange, it found out more about the places that its partners' users went to.

Such developments marked Foursquare's progression from a fun app that plugged into sites like Facebook and Twitter to a full-fledged social network in its own right. In 2010, Facebook, Microsoft and Yahoo! had courted Foursquare for an estimated US$100 million while the app had barely a million users. An estimated value of US$100 per user was unprecedented in the history of technology business. A couple of years, and millions of users later, Foursquare had become the poster child of second-generation location services. It had masterfully turned itself into a powerful mobile marketing tool for any brand—large or small—to participate in the mobile-centric social media revolution.

The challenge for Foursquare was that it needed to keep getting more people to use it like a daily utility, so it could make more money through its paid promoted updates. Foursquare was trying to help the process along by opening up its website as a local search tool to all users. Moreover, Foursquare's access to detailed purchase data bolstered its claims to be an effective tool for vendors trying to drum up local business. The local discovery stalwart, for example, could help make the places more meaningful by employing this massive amount of trending data or interest data. Foursquare's 30 million users would be able to sync their MasterCard and Visa credit and debit cards with the app. Those who did so would receive targeted discounts from participating merchants; Burger King and its 7,000-plus locations had signed on as the pilot partner.

The deals with MasterCard and Visa represented an extension of a partnership Foursquare had had with American Express since 2011. But the American Express deal was not revenue-generating, while with these partnerships, Foursquare would get paid on a cost-per-transaction basis. The deals to offer discounts to MasterCard and Visa cardholders with participating merchants being one way that Foursquare could earn commissions. The location service provider was clearly aiming to couple its service with a mobile commerce play—not just in the area of payments but in bringing would-be consumers into places where those payments would be made. And the possibilities for location-based services on mobile went beyond consumer-facing shopping and payment apps. With over 770 million GPS-enabled smartphones, location data had begun to permeate the entire mobile space. It was powering advertisements, and many other services—from weather to travel apps.

Location-based features were boosting the engagement for mobile apps and that in turn generated excitement for the location-enabled mobile ads. The simple fact of a user being physically close to a business, within two miles or so, gave a significant lift to click-through rates on mobile ads. Many mobile ad trading platforms were reporting triple-digit increases in location-enabled impressions. Advertisers could direct their spending toward transactional content that had a lot of intent and could easily convert to a purchase. That could win out over topical content found on Facebook and Twitter, which produced content with low signals. While the preceding chapters provided a detailed account of the mobile payment ecosystem, the following chapters will explore how local data could connect hundreds of thousands of businesses large and small to the mobile economy. The location layer of the Internet was about to transform the mobile ad paradigm.

# 8 THE GOLDEN AGE OF ADVERTISING

*"Whoever does mobile best, they're going to be the next Google, so people are asking, 'Is Google going to be the next Google?' It still is Google's to lose."*

— Chris Winfield, co-founder of BlueGlass Interactive, a digital advertising agency

The obstacles to making full use of location-aware data—summed up as the Starbucks dilemma—had haunted proponents since the beginning of the m-commerce dream. A mobile phone user walked by a popular coffee house and her device would recognize where it was and receive a coupon or discount in the form of push-notification from the coffee shop. This compelling blend of geo-fencing, push technology, and real-time marketing delivered straight to a mobile phone user explored the notion of proximity advertising. The idea had been around for almost two decades but was obviously very hard to put to fruition. That's because it required a set of building blocks that the first-generation location services simply couldn't deliver. However, by 2012, all the missing pieces of the puzzle in the "Starbucks dilemma" were falling into place to deliver this specialized form of targeted marketing.

Businesses had wanted this ability for decades but it was challenging to wade through a number of roadblocks—inventory and privacy being the primary barriers. Inventory problems were inevitable if businesses limited promotions to a small geographical area. However, with the Groupon effect, which persuaded small businesses into the online advertising world, inventory challenges gradually eased. As for the concerns over privacy, consumers wanted a transparent mechanism to know what type of information was being collected about them and how much of it was being exposed to advertisers. The industry needed to be very open about the data it collected and how it was to be used in order to ease mobile users' privacy concerns. Then there were rival mobile platforms like Android and iOS and mobile operators' competing agendas that caused so much fragmentation in the marketplace that mobile advertising was a non-starter for many years.

The notion of proximity advertising eventually began to gain traction with second-generation location services like Foursquare which facilitated social discovery in the local settings through check-in features. As explained in chapters 6 and 7, social discovery was made possible by the geo-fencing technology, which helped reach people when they entered a specific area and thus helped to route ads to specific locations like a grocery store or a coffee house. Check-in apps like Foursquare could help brands and retailers test new product concepts and build campaigns to drive foot traffic and ultimately more sales. What was driving the adoption of location-based marketing among brands and retailers was the desire to reach the right person at the right time for the right need. Marketers clearly saw the mobile ad upside of being personal and targeted as it promised a much higher ROI. Marketers could use location to target people by proximity and then send them an offer that appealed specifically to their needs.

Location and granular geo-targeting were strong predictors of consumer intent because where mobile users were said a lot about what they might be interested in. Consumers were now beginning to use their phones for every stage of the purchase cycle—locating stores, researching products, reading peer reviews, and looking for coupons. So it was apparent to retailers that location-based services were an important key to driving foot traffic among consumers who were in the midst of making a purchase. In addition, location-based mobile marketing was all about relevancy and communicating a clear value proposition to the brand's target audience. Adding the location component to a campaign gave marketers the opportunity to increase the relevancy of their messages and made them immediately actionable. There was a broad consensus that once the privacy conundrum was resolved, for instance, by gaining mobile users' explicit permission, location-based mobile services could provide tangible benefits to both the retailer and the consumer.

# THE LOCAL ADVERTISING

Reaching consumers was a big part of the game, but it was only a start. The ultimate goal was to generate transactions, and that's where relevance through mobile became significant. Tying into the context of the consumer—location, time of day, etc.—improved the relevancy. People were generally far more receptive to ads that were relevant to them personally. It was only natural that mobile consumers would be more inclined to interact with the ad to redeem a coupon or earn loyalty points, once they were nearby a particular store or restaurant of their choice. So adding location or geo-targeting to a marketing campaign could lead to higher click-throughs and actions because that campaign became locally relevant for specific mobile phone users.

Location was a big deal in mobile advertising because it leveraged the mobility of smartphones and tablets; it reached consumers when they were out and about, on the go, interacting with both the digital and real worlds.It fulfilled the longstanding goal of "right ad, right person, right place, and right time." The location data enabled attributes like user intent, demographics and audience segments, and thus brought genuine value to mobile users by helping them find products and services where and when they wanted them. Not surprisingly, therefore, agencies and brands saw enormous potential in location targeting, and consequently, technology companies started building the next-generation platforms for harvesting and leveraging this data for marketing and advertising.

However, the early efforts had been slower to take off, in part because ads delivered via geo-fencing or proximity data didn't necessarily catch people at a time when they wanted to act or didn't factor in a person's preferences. The market had been flooded with bad location data. There were many sources for actionable mobile location data. The device could share GPS level data which was typically represented by latitude and longitude coordinates (lat/long) and was generally very accurate. The network could share data derived from cellular tower triangulation which was also quite accurate. There was also user-supplied location data; a user, for instance, provided his zip code when registering for a site or service.

Another method of deriving location was IP address analysis, which could range from very accurate to completely inaccurate. An IP lookup could be helpful in Wi-Fi environments where locations like an airport or coffee shop were well indexed, but mobile operator locations were accurate only to the metro or zip level. The targeted mobile advertising campaigns, on the other hand, were focused on targeting people in an area the size of a city block, a shopping center or a big box store and required precise lat/long data. The lat/long data was very scarce. Industry experts estimated that about 5 to 10 percent of mobile ad impressions had lat/long data from users who had opted in to share location with an app or mobile site. Many of the popular gaming and Internet radio apps, for instance, weren't allowed by Apple to ask for location.

Another challenge in location-based advertising was that some publishers made up the lat/long data to move the needle in mobile ad exchanges. Some ad exchanges and networks claimed 70, 80 or even 100 percent lat/long impressions in 2012 when 5 to 10 percent of all mobile impressions had lat/long data. There were two primary techniques used to generate "inferred" lat/longs: centroid and randomized lat/longs. Centroids were lat/long coordinates that were generated by software programs that automatically picked the center of a geographic region as a substitute for either no location data or for lesser-quality location data. Randomized lat/longs were generated by software programs that randomly chose lat/longs within a region.

Such bogus location data threatened the evolution of the highly granular location targeting that had so much potential and had marketers got so excited. The inferred lat/longs drove down performance by targeting the wrong place and the wrong people. Location targeting in mobile had enormous promise, but the lack of transparency in location data was holding things back. Moreover, it was technically challenging to track mobile users and deliver relevant audience demographics. That's because the fragmented mobile landscape lacked the common standards and protocols that enabled relatively seamless ad delivery and measurement on desktop.

Local ads could become a substantial part of the market once inventory and demand could be matched up at the precise moment. Brands and retailers were apparently keen to incorporate mobile ads into their marketing campaigns but these issues needed to be worked out for wireless ads to reach critical mass. The premise of location-targeted ads had always been attractive to marketers, but at the same time, it'd been hard to execute.

Eventually, technology platforms began to emerge to provide a measure of transparency to counter the problem of "inferred" lat/longs. They used city, zip, user supplied or IP targeted location data to help mobile advertisers recognize and parse ad impressions with genuine location data from those with false location data and cherry pick verified impressions. Startup companies such as Verve were cultivating their business on legitimate location data. Then there were upstarts like Sense, JiWire and WHERE who were getting smarter about mixing location data with behavioral profiles to deliver more relevant ads to people.

The Starbucks dilemma embodied the struggles of the first-generation location technology. But with the advent of second-generation location services like Foursquare, marketers could tie their message to a specific place and tailor the context of the message according to the location. Foursquare and other second-generation location startups had taken the first good step to realize the dream of proximity advertising. Location-based mobile advertising could now fulfill the long-held promise of delivering marketing content in the right place at the right time with the right message.

Before this the wireless ad networks didn't know much about location and context-aware campaign management. The entire mobile ad infrastructure needed to reconfigure itself to handle location- and context-aware campaign management. The marketing message would change from street to street and that meant a huge shift in ad inventory management. For that, brands and retailers would need to be equipped with the right tools that helped them craft and modify marketing messages with change in location and context.

In location-based ads, there was also a danger in being too pushy, thus creeping out users who didn't know their location was being tracked. It was imperative that mobile advertising challenged the notion that it indiscriminately sprayed users. Location was a critical aspect of mobile ads as demonstrated in this section. The upcoming sections will delve into the mobile advertising segment at large and will explain how this industry was becoming a crucial part of the mobile commerce juggernaut.

# APP AS AN AD

If the premise of m-commerce was for real, it wouldn't be long before everything in the business world would be linked to the wireless Internet and would be remotely controlled via mobile phones. This very epitome of m-commerce, in turn, brought forth an exciting and enticing idea to the mobile frontier: wireless ads. A couple of years after the m-commerce hype took hold, the notion of wireless advertising surfaced as a way to reach people wherever they were and in a way that was both personal and relevant. For instance, people would walk down the street to a chorus of beeps and rings as coupons and ads from nearby shops arrive at their wireless inboxes. The proponents said that such manifestation of wireless technology could revamp century-old advertising business by bringing powerful features like interactivity and pay-for-performance. In many ways, America was initially persuading m-commerce experiment mostly from a wireless ads perspective.

In the early 2000s, the mobile industry saw a modest degree of trials of interactive branding ads. The supporters of wireless ads had reckoned that personalized push technology, rather than simple web surfing, would keep mobile phone users informed on the road. That premise in fact led analysts to predict that m-commerce would become a trillion-dollar business by the mid-2000s. Industry at large had also accepted the public-relations hyperbole of handset manufacturers and wireless network operators on how a myriad of innovative ad services could be delivered over the mobile devices. It sounded like a great idea for advertisers and wireless operators, but could become a nightmare for consumers, many of whom were already fending off a growing torrent of junk e-mails on their PCs.

At this juncture of the m-commerce evolution, the whole idea of wireless ads looked more like a paradox because shopping, by definition, seemed more about wandering. Mobile phone companies at the forefront of wireless ad campaigns were evidently making some of the most egregious errors. They were not only harming their subscribers but also credibility of the entire wireless data movement by embracing such an inept form of advertising. Fast-forward to late 2000s: Apple had reshaped the mobile Internet world and, within that periphery, mobile commerce. Once the iPhone accompanied with the power of apps got into the game, the whole landscape changed. The smartphone emerged as a powerful new advertising platform and now industry watchers began to wonder if the App Store could do for mobile ads what iTunes did for music and video.

"The iPhone was the first mobile device with a good web browser, and more such devices will follow," said then-Google CEO Eric Schmidt. "Advertising will then become very personal. In a few years, mobile advertising will generate more revenue than advertising on the normal web." But if mobile devices took over as the computing platform for consumers, then Google's web advertising channel, and the heart of its revenue, would be gutted. It didn't take much of a crystal ball to see where Apple was going and it was not a pretty picture for Google. If the enigma surrounding Android and how the new economy bellwether would make money out of its mobile foray could be unraveled, the key to that had to be somewhere at this very junction in the m-commerce trail. A proof of how crucial mobile advertising space was in Google's scheme of things came in November 2009 when the company announced the acquisition of AdMob, the leading mobile advertising company.

AdMob allowed advertisers to create and target banner and text ads across mobile websites and apps with plenty of detail. AdMob—a marketplace that connected advertisers with mobile publishers—allowed ads be targeted to locations, mobile phone platforms, wireless operators, and handset manufacturers. Ads could also be targeted to specific mobile sites or mobile users could browse their channel categories like communities, contextual search, entertainment, etc. All ads ran on auction-based pricing system.

Until 2010, the mobile advertising business was a small fraction of the US$25 billion U.S. online advertising market. Apple's cachet with big brands helped legitimize the entire market and spurred marketers to boost their spending in interactive mobile ads category. But even with Apple's successful purpose-built iOS platform designed to support the apps that ran on its smart devices, it could be a long way from creating the sort of broad-based advertising platform that defined Google's forte on wired web. So when Google outbid Apple to purchase AdMob for US$750 million, Apple followed by buying one of AdMob's competitors, Quattro Wireless. AdMob's nemesis, Quattro Wireless, founded in 2006, eventually helped Apple create the iAd experience for in-app mobile advertising system incorporated in its mobile operating system iOS. Unlike hard-to-read miniature text ads, the rich media ads of the iAd featured interactive elements and slick video and animation.

The smartphone market was a prize in itself; what both Apple and Google were after was the wireless ad market that the leadership in the smartphone business could facilitate. The integration of a mobile ad network into Google's larger infrastructure was a testament to the web titan's quest for revenue stream beyond its core search business. Apple, on the other hand, was promoting rich media ads, which kept users within an application instead of transporting them somewhere else. These ads let mobile consumers play a mini-game or interact with the ad without having to leave or the close the app they were using. "We have figured out how to do interactive video content without ever taking you out of the apps," Steve Jobs told the audience at the launch of the iAd platform. "We think people are going to be a lot more interested in clicking on these things."

In 2010, Apple stepped up its rivalry with Google by adding its own advertising system to the next version of iOS that powered the iPhone, the iPad, and other mobile gadgets. Apple's iAd mobile advertising platform let advertisers make inventive messages appear inside apps. Apple would sell the ads, with developers who created the apps getting 60 percent of the revenue of any mobile ad, and Apple taking the remainder. Jobs emphasized the new ad platform's immersive, interactive and emotional aspects, which enabled developers and advertisers to include animation, video, and rich graphics inherently integrated within the iOS platform. So, for instance, users could click on an ad to add a new wallpaper image to their iPhones. Ads were built using HTML5, a not-so-indirect jab at Adobe's Flash platform, which was widely used to provide interactivity and animation in web ads but was not supported on the iOS software.

Apple's entry into the market through the acquisition of Quattro, and subsequently the inception of iAd, had put a spotlight on mobile advertising. Application developers, a key part of this equation, acknowledged that iAd platform for the iPhone and iPad applications had provided them with a new channel to monetize their software products. Add to that 4 billion iPhone app downloads, 3.5 million iPad app downloads, and 64 percent of smartphone mobile browser usage share and the iAd opportunity could sell itself. Moreover, the iAd's richer ad units and higher click-through rates were complemented by the iPhone and iPad ecosystem, in which to buy a certain item took a single click using a credit card linked to an iTunes account.

## ANATOMY OF MOBILE AD

Apple constrained adoption of the service by requiring a very expensive minimum spending commitment from advertisers that was dramatically slashed later on. The Cupertino, California–based company announced it was lowering the buy-in price for iAds from US$500,000 to US$100,000 and increasing the publisher revenue share from 60 percent to 70 percent. It was chilling for many industry watchers to see Apple in an unfamiliar role of making compromises on price in an attempt to revive iAd. The move marked a sense of inferiority and showed that while mobile advertisement was huge in potential, it was still lumbering and not mature.

Even the independent mobile advertising company Millennial Media was able to top Apple's market share. By early 2012, Millennial served ads to 200 million mobile users worldwide; more than 30,000 apps were enabled to receive ads delivered by Millennial. One of the largest remaining independent wireless ad networks was helping the mobile display advertising marketplace grow by becoming the preferred partner to advertisers seeking to reach mobile customers; to application and media developers seeking to maximize app revenue; and to wireless operators wanting to further monetize. So what went wrong in Apple's gleaming world of iAd? First and foremost, ad guys didn't like to be told by a technology company how to market to consumers. If advertising folks couldn't run ads the way they wanted on iPhone, iPad and iPod touch, they would probably be happy to run them on Android or independent mobile ad platforms like Millennial.

While Apple limited itself to its proprietary platform, which apparently led to a sense of lack of control among marketers, pushing many of them to rival products, there were deeper issues in the mobile ad conundrum. Major players like Apple, Google, and Millennial were trying to reinvent advertising in the age of the apps, but they confronted a serious dilemma. A closer look at how ad networks implemented in-app software to deliver advertising to mobile consumers—and help developers get paid—revealed a peculiar relationship between app developer and ad network. An intimate examination of running ads and how the ads interacted with the app, mobile device, and user data also led to worrisome findings for users who were sensitive to being tracked by advertisers.

Application developers connected to ad networks through special piece of software within an app which formed a sublevel to the app that developers didn't necessarily control. Given the nature of the special relationship between app and ad network, an ad could effectively leverage all the information by inheriting permissions a user granted to the app. These were permissions that allowed apps the use of certain user data and they were mostly explicit to the mobile user. So, by using an ad-supported app, a mobile user gave permission to the advertiser to use information gathered through use of the app. Thus, even when an app didn't cost money, it wasn't really free. Part of the price that mobile users paid was by giving up their data so that marketers could send ads to them. That undermined the app-based privacy and security safeguards and genuinely concerned many people. Consequently, the issues of invasively collecting personal information and permissively disclosing data to running ads put the mobile ad industry in a state of flux.

In general, people didn't want to be tracked and didn't want advertisers to identify them or their behavior. But the ability to know everything possible about a person produced advertising power that marketers never had before. Ads that knew a user's location and general behavior could be beneficial to people as long as there was a reliable and privacy-conscious tracking mechanism for networks and developers to better target users. The desktop-based e-commerce world came to a similar crossroads in the mid-1990s when online advertisers were trying to figure out the power of tracking user behavior on the web. After a number of hits and misses, the industry settled on a first-party cookie tracking mechanism as a solution that balanced consumer and commercial needs. Advertisers could use the cookies to find out where a user was, what websites he frequented, and target advertising to him. Conversely, users could block cookies if they wanted.

It was the standard method of tagging, tracking, and targeting online ads. The cookie was a small text file that websites stored on a given computer's web browser which subsequently identified it. But cookies didn't work as reliably or powerfully on the web browsers of mobile devices, and there was no such thing as a cookie inside a mobile app, where much of people's time was spent. The technologies for tracking users and measuring the impact of ads hadn't kept up with consumers' fast switch to smartphones and tablets, leaving marketers unsure if the ads were working. So advertisers remained unwilling to commit large budgets. They didn't know if the ads were working, like they did on personal computers. Media channels depended critically upon reliable metrics for audience reach, but here, mobile ads were challenged by serious methodological and technological limitations.

# GOOGLE ON TOP

While Apple tried to contain mobile advertising in its controlled universe, Google was happy to run ads on any mobile device with a browser. The Internet giant was also vindicated in its fervor for the purchase data now viewed as a treasure trove for marketers; mobile ad firms were now starting to use it to promote special offers and deals. The fact that Google was making barely a ripple with its mobile wallet offering made headlines in tech media, but that missed the point. Google was selling ads across all digital channels, from search to banners to television. And providing its wallet service free of charge suggested that Google was really after user data which would subsequently boost its mobile advertising business.

Plugging the purchase data into the mobile wallet might turbo-charge the Groupon-style offers and deals, especially if the consumer was incentivized to opt-in and provide his real-time location. Google, for instance, could run ads for Burger King to people who had purchased at McDonalds, and ads for McDonald's at Burger King. It was easy to track when a paid search link resulted in an online hotel booking, but it wasn't that easy to track when a paid search ad resulted in the purchase of a cheeseburger. That's where the purchase data from tap-to-pay transactions through Google's mobile wallet could be of huge value.

The fact that apps like Google Maps and Gmail helped make the iPhone the best mobile handset on the planet made many wonder why would Google help its archrival Apple. The answer boiled down to advertising. In the bigger scheme of things,

Android and even Motorola handset division were sideshows to Google's ad business. Google pumped money into Android to ensure that companies like Apple and Microsoft couldn't push their properties into smartphone business. Android's another major aim was to create the economy of scale in smartphone business by reducing the prices since smartphones were complements of Google's web-based services. Google didn't make money from its Android platform; it made money when people used Google services.

It's worthwhile to note that Google withheld turn-by-turn directions from the data it supplied to Apple's infamous Maps app released during the launch of iPhone 5 in September 2012. Apple controlled the front-end of that app and Google was a mere back-end supplier, so there was no ad sales opportunity for Google. The new version of Google Maps on the iPhone 5 was a standalone product and there was the potential for ads, so turn-by-turn directions had been included. The Android version of Google Maps already contained ads. Apps like Google Maps not only did know where mobile users were, they also knew where they were going and what types of businesses they were looking for, the sort of intention data advertisers found invaluable. Gmail for iOS was similarly a big potential driver of advertising; the web version of the app had already had ads targeted based on the content of e-mail messages.

Google's lead in the mobile ad space was owed to its powerful search franchise and Android platform. In 2011, Google captured more than half of U.S. mobile ad revenues, accounting for 95 percent of the mobile search ad market and 25 percent of the mobile display market. Next year, in 2012, according to eMarketer, Google earned 56 percent of all mobile ad dollars and 96 percent of mobile search ad dollars. The issues outlined in the previous section mostly relate to display-style and banner-style mobile ads. Search-based mobile ads, on the other hand, were doing a lot better. There was ample evidence to suggest that search ads were working even better on tablets and smartphones than they did on desktop platforms. Mobile searches were quickly becoming the main way in which users found everything they needed, whether it was information, services, or physical goods.

Mobile search could be a lot closer to the purchase point than a desktop search and thus could be more valuable and competitive. Mobile search was also valuable for advertisers because most users were very intent-driven when they searched on a mobile phone and were likely to complete a task after searching. With a phone in hand, a mobile user was probably more likely to be ready to buy something. People searching for jeans on a desktop, for instance, most likely wanted to research styles and colors, while people doing the same search on a phone wanted the nearest place to buy a pair. Mobile phones knew a lot more about people than desktop computers did—most important, their location. According to Google, nine out of ten mobile searches by users had resulted in an action such as a purchase or a visit to a business.

Given that Google was the default search engine on iOS and Android—which represented around 80 percent of the global smartphone market as of 2012—its dominance was not surprising. The digital media giant had effectively monopolized the mobile search market. It dominated the paid search category which accounted for 62 percent of mobile global ad spending in 2012. The Google data also showed that 30 percent of restaurant searches and 25 percent of movie searches were done on mobile devices. Google's mobile search ad revenues accounted for 5 percent of all paid search in 2011. Next year, in 2012, Google expected mobile devices to account for 25 percent of its paid search ad clicks.

Google search, obviously, was well-suited to the mobile medium. However, while the majority of the money Google made on the mobile side was from mobile search, a good chunk of that came from the iPhone. So far, the Android mobile platform had not been a significant money maker for Google, either directly or indirectly. For Google, AdWords was still the most valuable platform because the search giant had not been able to monetize Android in a way that was satisfactory. Given that Google's web search advertising business was becoming less dominant in the age of mobile, it was imperative for Google to reclaim lost desktop dollars as people moved to mobile.

Moreover, mobile ad networks, demand side platforms, mobile ad exchanges were all part of a dynamic ecosystem that was constantly evolving and trying to grow non-search mobile related advertising. While Google pretty much owned the mobile search category in the early going, local search engines like AroundMe and location-based services like Foursquare could threaten Google as more mobile users got their mobile queries answered through dedicated apps. Consumers were searching more on apps vertically focused on specific categories like shopping and restaurants. That included location-aware searches, which were increasing outside of Google's ecosystem.

Google was the world's largest seller of online ads and had an in-depth understanding of the online ad business. Making mobile advertising work was crucial for Google because consumers were spending more time on phones than desktop. Google, its Android licensees, and its rivals had been trying to crack the mobile advertising market and figure out how to make money selling ads on mobile devices. And each one of them was taking a different approach toward finding a solution. Apple was working on it. Facebook was working on it. So Google knew it needed to figure this out before somebody like Facebook came and did it.

## MOBILE MARKETING TIPPING POINT

The holy grail of marketers used to be a home telephone number and address. Direct mail and telemarketing, despite being some of the most hated forms of advertising, had been historically effective. Now mobile took marketers closer to consumers than landline telephone and direct mail ever could. Mobile was also poised to surpass television as the dominant consumer access point. The era of broadcasting a message with a one-size-fits-all approach was gradually fading and could well be taken over by short, relevant and timely nuggets of information unique to each user. Marketing the way people know it could become another victim in the smartphone's coming-of-age story. How people experienced life, relationships, entertainment, education, exercise, and work had been completely transformed because of mobile, for better or worse.

In the 1960s, agencies controlled a brand's message and how it was broadcast to an extremely broad target audience on a small number of platforms. Things had changed a lot since then. In the year 2000, London hosted the first symposium on mobile marketing. Next, in the post-iPhone age, everyone's roles were blurred and traditional agency conventions were being challenged to keep pace with ever-changing client demands. The early doubts about whether people wanted ads splashed on their mobile handset screens were clearly fading. Despite all the challenges related to privacy and other aspects of advertising value chain, the only way was up for the mobile ad movement because of the smartphone's superior features like apps and rich media.

An advertiser could buy an ad in a famous magazine like *Cosmopolitan*, but there were a lot of people that didn't read magazines. On the other hand, people were on their mobile phones constantly. So a shift was inevitable from the old, network-heavy mobile ads to new types of distribution deals and controls of ad inventory through a new generation of platforms and services. This was probably the most exciting and unpredictable time in the marketing history. The golden age of mobile was here and would be here for years. While the ad-spend numbers didn't quite match the potential growth, this chapter attempted to gather all the evidence on how the marketing industry was actually beginning to enter the golden age of mobile and that the ad spending would follow with eventual mobile ubiquity. Case in point: digital media giant Facebook had been building out its mobile arsenal with the acquisitions such as Instagram, Glancee, and Karma.

This was the dawn of the smartphone age. But it wasn't evident by simply looking at mobile ad budgets. There was still a huge gap between the rapid adoption of mobile and the ad budgets assigned to it. However, not having a mobile strategy and roadmap in place for businesses could be a recipe for disruption. Most of the corporate resources and innovation were now focused toward building apps and delivering them through various mobile marketing channels. Location and payment services—as chronicled in chapters 4, 5, 6 and 7—as well as mobile ads mostly relied on the power of apps. And the industry was a witness of how apps disrupted multi-billion dollar businesses—gaming, retail, media, publishing, small business, photography, and travel.

However, while people were actually spending more time on their mobile devices than they were on the traditional web, the industry observers kept pondering on why mobile advertising had attracted only a tiny fraction of ad spending. Ad performance and user engagement went hand in hand. Mobile users would engage more deeply with ads if they were fun and rewarding for users to click on, and that would require a renewed effort on a reward-based advertising platform. Then there was the open playing field of what social networks could make of mobile ads. On a larger scale, mobile demanded a unique approach to advertising and that precise recipe was a work in progress. No wonder mass market advertising had been hesitant to make big bets on a market that was changing as quickly as mobile.

Mobile advertising didn't become the bonanza it was supposed to be. It had been a bit slow off the ground, and its growth trajectory was not clear as of 2013. According to 2012 estimates from eMarketer, an advertising research company, U.S. adults spent about 82 minutes a day on average using mobile devices for activities other than calls. Yet only about 2 percent of all advertising dollars was being spent on mobile websites or inside mobile apps. The next chapter, while lining up new bright spots in the mobile ad industry, also takes a microscopic look at why ad dollars were not following the consumers' attention that otherwise increasingly went toward the mobile world.

# MOBILE AD'S CINDERELLA MOMENT

*"It's reminiscent of the web in 1996 and 1997. People weren't interested in ads, and prices were low. But advertisers don't have a choice. They've got to go where audiences are."*

— Michael Moritz, a venture capitalist at
Sequoia Capital

In the early stage, mobile ads mostly remained just miniature versions of ads on websites, like the early days of the Internet when advertisers essentially slapped print ads online. But eventually, advertisers began tailoring ads to phones by taking advantage of elements like their ability to track location, make a call, show maps with directions and add calendar alerts. One of the early breakthroughs in the mobile ad space hadn't been flashy advertisement but making calls by clicking on ads. In 2010, Google introduced an innovative new form of advertising that could be tapped to make a call. This was how it worked. A mobile phone user in a strange city searched for hotels on Google and saw a nearby one listed at the top of the rankings, with a little phone icon that said, "Call." He tapped it, reached the hotel and asked for a room. The icon was the so-called click-to-call ad, and the hotel paid Google when a mobile user called. Just like that, Google made money.

Google's click-to-call ads became a new form of sales call and lead generation. The click-to-call business—a form of voice communications using online data service—quickly became a bright spot for the embryonic mobile ad industry by producing higher click-through rates. A phone call initiated on a website was a hit with businesses who wanted to reach an online audience; plumbers and pizzerias loved click-to-call because it let them reach customers at the right place and at the right time. Companies like 1-800-Flowers said that customers were two to three times more likely to click to make a phone call from a handset than to click on advertisements on a desktop computer. Google's click-to-call ad became one of the most successful mobile ad types because it sought a new way to reach consumers and exploited the smaller mobile screen with an inventive mechanism.

Next up, voice-recognition software maker Nuance began developing a way for mobile users to chat with ads much as they did with Siri on the iPhone. Nuance, founded in 1994, was known to have provided technology that powered Apple's Siri app. Its Voice Ads technology, which worked off the Internet connection of any iOS or Android mobile device, was made available on mobile ad networks like Jumptap, Millennial

Media, and Opera Mediaworks. However, initially, the mobile ad technology wasn't supported in third-party rich-media ad creation tools, except Celtra, and ad developers had to work directly with Nuance to connect the advertising to the company's voice-recognition servers over the Internet. Just like click-to-call ads, these voice ads saved mobile users from fiddling on tiny links or trying to type on a 4-inch screen. Moreover, such ads allowed mobile users to have a live conversation with a brand and thus make a brand feel more responsive.

Most mobile ads were initially search and display ads viewed on mobile. But then mobile video ads got on a roll, hitting 100 million views in August 2012, more than a year after they were debuted by Flurry on Apple's iOS platform. Android was apparently Flurry's next destination to reach mobile users with TV-style commercial videos. Advertisers could use video, animation, photo galleries and interactive elements, which made mobile advertising more akin to a TV commercial or a slick magazine. These ads appeared as rich multimedia content that started after a mobile user clicked on a prompt. The videos allowed traditional advertisers to reach consumers at a fraction of the cost of TV commercials. The inception of these ads reflected not only the more engaging nature of video but also the rise of tablet use, which lent itself to more video viewing. Mobile video ads also provided app developers with an effective way to drive download of their apps.

Mobile video ads were taking off for three reasons. First, faster LTE-based 4G networks, along with larger screens and faster processors in smartphones, were driving more video consumption. Second, the YouTube generation of young users was adopting mobile video habits far more quickly. Third, tablets with bigger and higher-resolution screens did the heavy lifting for mobile video and favored mobile video playback. By 2012, although there were far fewer tablets in the market than smartphones, tablets accounted for 3.7 percent of all online video hours watched globally, compared to 4.5 percent for smartphones.

The rise of video ads was crucial for the entire mobile ecosystem. According to Opera Software, the mobile browser company, advertisers had started using rich media and video ads more frequently than traditional banner ads in 2012. Moreover, according to a report from video advertising platform provider Videology, mobile video impressions saw an 84 percent hike in the fourth quarter of 2012, taking the total to 18.6 million. Audio ads provided the next immersive experience in the mobile space. Pandora—the Internet radio service—was second only to Google in mobile ad revenue from both audio and on-screen ads in 2012. An audio ad, for instance, told Pandora listeners to tap the screen for the location of the nearest Japanese restaurant and grab a sushi lunch special.

## THE UDID JUNCTION

At this very juncture, when the industry was tackling some of the unsolved problems in mobile advertising, Apple threw a stunner. The company announced that to ensure mobile user privacy it would deprecate the unique device identifier or UDID feature and thus pre-empt advertisers and analytics services from tracking user behavior. UDID was an anonymized number connected to an iOS device that publishers and advertisers could use to track user behavior and better target ads to those users. In Apple's mobile ecosystem, UDID was the most effective solution for mobile advertisers because it provided trackers a lot of useful information about the user. It helped track a mobile user's identity and location with information like the user's birth date, gender, e-mail address, etc. UDID was a one-stop shop for most of the analytics needs for allowing developers and advertisers to target advertising, send relevant push notifications, and prompt users to open an app.

However, the fact that it allowed advertisers to get some of the most granular data of a user also raised privacy alarm bells. Apple began enforcing the move away from UDIDs in late 2011 and introduced the Advertising Identifier in September 2012. Advertising Identifier let users have more privacy and gave them more control over what publishers and advertisers knew about their use of apps. The mobile advertisement industry was very close to its Cinderella moment when Apple's move to abandon UDID brought everything back to square one, or so said the pundits. They suspected that Apple was aiming to identify unique users through its iTunes database and could reserve the unique user information to itself as a trusted steward of consumer privacy.

In the intrinsic relationship between ads and apps, ads were served within apps by third-party providers—ad networks—who plugged ads into the app. In a rush to win a slice of the pie in this monstrous untapped opportunity called mobile advertising, free mobile apps began incorporating aggressive ads that not only invaded privacy, but also changed settings or delivered ads outside the context of apps. Slapping in ads proved to be a short-term solution that stunted the app's organic growth. When a mobile user was spending an average of 71 seconds on an app, the last thing on her mind was going to be whether she wanted to buy the latest detergent in the market. App developers didn't know much about how an ad network behaved when their ads were integrated into the apps. In a dash to make their apps profitable, developers used the ad network that offered the biggest payoff, regardless of what that might mean for users.

Many developers eventually realized that and placed a price on downloading their apps, especially for non-media apps. Still, advertising was an important part of delivering free apps to users; app developers needed to get paid or their apps wouldn't be available. While ad networks needed to hold user privacy in the highest regard and be as clear and straightforward as possible in their practices to the end user, app developers just couldn't trust ad networks to do the right thing. They needed to educate themselves on the ins and outs of ad delivery and network behavior. For that, a simple way to track user habits made it easier for developers to understand user behavior and in some cases to target users with ads.

Mobile ad buyers wanted to see a vibrant ecosystem of ads, and for that, the mobile advertisement business would have to evolve in a way that was acceptable for consumers. However, the truth was that phone manufacturers, wireless operators, and mobile OS software providers had created a fragmented and feature-poor cookie environment on mobile handsets. Moreover, mobile ecosystems had a tendency to benefit ad networks in a way that also created a set of loopholes and thus could give mobile users a pause. Privacy issues genuinely concerned people and it was about time that mobile ecosystems addressed the lack of ad infrastructure and helped create a reliable, privacy-conscious tracking mechanism that all ad networks and app developers could use. Moreover, analytics, measurement, and targeting in the mobile world had not caught up with the online counterpart. There was, for instance, a need for better modeling to determine which mobile users were likely to fall into a specific demographic and to target ads based on those predictions.

The projected rapid evolution of mobile commerce between 2012 and 2017 was reckoned to be predominately driven by an increase in the number of mobile buyers, which would be of specific interest to retailers and mobile advertisers. By 2012 the industry was already witnessing a seismic shift from desktops to mobile. But while mobile had a tremendous potential as an advertising medium, the question was when would advertisers catch up? Mobile ads offered a unique power as a one-to-one communication channel, but were consumers paying attention? The truth was that, with the explosion in mobile adoption, there had been a lot more supply of mobile ad inventory than demand. On the other hand, marketers had been mostly slow to embrace mobile, out of inertia or lack of education. While mobile traffic was growing rapidly, most marketers still believed desktop ads were worth about five times the mobile equivalent.

In 2012, people spent about 10 percent of their time on mobile devices, as pointed out by Kleiner Perkins partner Mary Meeker, but only 1 percent of U.S. ad budget went to mobile. Compare that to the largely struggling print medium that attracted only about 7 percent of media time, but still captured an astonishing 25 percent of the total U.S. ad spend—twenty five-times more ad money than mobile. But this disparity between the two mediums gave a strong indication as to how much room mobile still had to grow. The gap between the amount of time people spent on mobile devices versus the amount of money advertisers spent there had to close eventually and that was a massive opportunity. It showed a big potential upside to mobile advertising once the content and quality of ads began to catch up. According to Meeker, the opportunity was worth roughly US$20 billion.

As noted by Meeker—a former Morgan Stanley analyst also known as the Queen of the Internet—there was a major mobile monetization gap, with eCPMs five times lower on mobile than on the desktop Internet. Even though Google's ad revenue continued to climb, the amount that advertisers paid for each click was falling, in part because there were more mobile ads that were worthless. The average cost an advertiser paid to show an ad to a thousand people on a desktop computer was US$3.50, but it was only 75 cents on mobile devices, according to estimates from the venture capital firm Kleiner, Perkins, Caufield, and Byers. Google, which dominated the US$70-billion-a-year business of digital ads, said that its average revenue from each ad click dipped 6 percent in 2012, a drop it attributed partly to users shifting to mobile devices.

Eventually, Google decided to bridge that gap with the biggest integration of its AdMob acquisition into the AdWords marketing platform. Google would assimilate AdMob into the larger AdWords ecosystem so that anyone buying web ads through AdWords could also buy them on mobile devices served by AdMob. Google was essentially forcing advertisers to design campaigns around context rather than specific device types. The company that brought search advertising to an enormous scale thanks in large part to AdWords' simple, self-serve model was attempting to solve the mobile monetization problem by enabling advertisers to manage all of their campaigns from a single interface.

From their AdWords dashboard, for example, advertisers could choose to have their display ads appear in mobile apps. They could target specific device models, manufacturers, or app categories featured on Google Play and Apple App Store. The AdWords campaigns on AdMob platform would initially cover cost-per-click campaigns and would incorporate CPM campaigns later. By 2012 AdWords had reached 2 million websites accessible by computers and boasted 1 million advertisers. Add 350 million Android mobile devices and 300,000 mobile apps to the AdWords universe and Google had a massive new market and potentially a larger demand for its mobile ad inventory.

## MOBILE AD ECOSYSTEM

The migration to mobile was not without challenges for ad sellers but the shakeup in the mobile ad norms was inevitable. If there was one statistic that described the massive untapped opportunity that was mobile advertising, it was the number of feature phones, also known in the mobile industry as dumb phones. There were approximately 6 billion devices—only handling calls and text messages—on the market as of 2012.

But though these feature phones outnumbered roughly 1 billion smartphones by a huge margin, they were inevitably going to be replaced by smartphones during upgrade cycles over the coming years. Imagine a world in 2015, where smartphones will be in the hands of almost every consumer and tablet sales will exceed PCs. According to Meeker, in 2012, there were 1.1 billion 3G mobile subscribers and they were increasing at a startling rate of 37 percent per year. So in the next three years, the number of global Internet users would double, fuelled by the increasingly ubiquitous presence of smartphones and mobile data usage.

Many marketers were held back from aggressively jumping onto mobile ads due to an apparent absence of clear ROI. Presenting ads was hard enough on a desktop—it only got harder when the real estate shrank. While ad buyers thought that mobile screens were too small for effective advertising, at the same time, many consumers found mobile ads invasive. So, despite the exponential growth in the number of smartphones and tablets, making money from mobile ads had proved extremely difficult. Moreover, the mobile ad ecosystem was not as strictly delineated as the desktop ecosystem and the rules of the game changed with different combinations of device, wireless operator, and operating system. Mobile lacked the technical consensus that enabled ad targeting, delivery, and measurement to work fairly seamlessly across the desktop world. There were innumerable actors interacting with one another and attempting to find a niche.

Another key barrier was the common perception that the future of mobile advertising was in display ads. The notion of putting fully-capable, interactive billboards in people's pockets through phones equipped with high-speed Internet connections and lightening fast processors didn't go far with the failure of high-profile projects like iAd. Even Millennial, another large ad network after Google and Apple, was struggling to make money. Tapping on these teeny-tiny bits in pop-ups required an annoying amount of precision, so users generally ignored the ad content. The gap in mobile ad spending versus the enormous time spent on mobile was real, and it existed partially because of these unappealing little ads. Banner displays were initially most popular ad units in mobile, but in terms of ad spending, they were eclipsed by search ads in the early 2010s. Display ads were prominent, in part because advertisers could buy in standard formats, like they were used to doing online. But the units were problematic on small screens because they could trigger more accidental clicks.

On the other hand, if advertisers kept the banners small to avoid turning off users, they could run into another problem: they were not engaging enough and thus easier for readers to ignore. Advertisers paid less for mobile ads than for those online, largely because mobile users were less likely to make a purchase on their phones. Though people clicked on mobile ads more than on desktop ads, advertisers wondered whether that was because of what they called the "fat finger effect"— accidental clicks on mobile ads because mobile screens were tiny. According to a 2012 study by Trademob, a German mobile-marketing company, accidental and false clicks made up 40 percent of all clicks on mobile ads. Some of the fraud came from app developers who generated false clicks from their servers; another method, similar to what happened on the Internet, deployed bot networks in which false clicks appeared to be coming from different IP addresses.

Google, the biggest sellers of mobile ads, vowed to fight back against the fat finger effect by double-checking that the mobile user wanted to visit the advertiser's website before taking them there. Google verified that mobile users meant to click on the ad by asking them to click again on a button labeled "visit site." When clicks were accidental, they usually happened near the outer edge of the ad, when a fat finger intended to scroll through the app instead. Google was confident that while the new feature would decrease the number of clicks on mobile ads, it would increase the number of people who made a purchase or otherwise interacted with an advertiser after clicking.

The third major roadblock in the way of first-generation mobile ads was the lack of tracking and reporting data. But from 2010 onward, advertisers began to enjoy a robust palette of mobile tools to choose from to connect their messages and marketing experiences with their desired audiences, thanks to advancements in mobile ad units, mobile search, mobile apps, mobile websites, and SMS. A new breed of startups began to provide advertising technology and solutions that enabled brands, advertising agencies, mobile operators and media to implement highly targeted, interactive and measurable campaigns. Each of these mobile tools was now being successfully embraced by advertisers to drive brand awareness, consideration, purchases, and loyalty. Better ad tracking and fine-tuned audience data were gradually allowing ad buyers to see what worked and what didn't on mobile.

Take mobile app measurement and advertising platform Flurry, which allowed app marketers the ability to track the effectiveness of their mobile ad campaigns. The Flurry ad analytics service—working with the major ad networks—showed from where users arrived, which campaigns were effective, and what any given network's user base looked like over time. Next, Flurry launched the Marketplace service which offered app publishers and developers a way to sell their ad inventory while also giving them accurate data about their audience. The San Francisco–based analytics software maker claimed to have access to the user habits of 90 percent of all active smartphone and tablet users in the world. The company said it had access to information about 300,000 apps used on over 1 billion mobile devices. The whole idea of Flurry serving a one-stop shop for app developers and publishers boiled down to one simple premise: if publishers clearly understood who was using their apps and why, they could make better decisions about where to place their ads in real-time.

Technology startups were now rushing to fill the infrastructure gap that had so far prevented mobile ads from becoming truly valuable. A particularly vexing problem for advertisers was the way users frequently switched back and forth between their mobile devices and a PC when performing a task. That meant advertisers couldn't tell if their ad worked. Here, Drawbridge provided cross-device ad targeting technology which allowed marketers to follow consumers from one device to another. So far, marketers had been buying from ten to fifteen ad networks and they had little visibility into the types of users being returned.

As the market for smartphones and tablets boomed, so did the available mobile ad inventory, creating a huge surplus that was hard to manage. Here, mobile ad network Todacell claimed to solve the problem through its campaign optimization technology which helped marketers reach the right mobile users.

The startup was able to optimize advertiser campaign results in a way that mass ad networks couldn't. Todacell's optimization technology took into account the potential targeting attributes of a campaign—publishers, creative, device, location, geo-targeting and demographics—and figured out where the campaign was working best. This could be via clicks, click through rate, or conversions. It then automatically adjusted the campaign to send more eyeballs toward where the action was. Past performance was also taken into account so advertisers could forecast results to get off to the best start for a campaign. Todacell also offered a licensable ad platform so that apps could replace obtrusive, overlaid, and still-loading ads with glossy, full-screen interstitials that could complement marketing experiences.

Another startup—955 Dreams—answered mobile monetization woes through an end-to-end ad engine that came with built-in analytics. The next notable innovation in the evolving mobile ad ecosystem came from Towerstream Corp., an operator of Wi-Fi networks in urban areas like New York and San Francisco. The wireless networking firm envisioned an auction system for selling location-based ads on its base stations; the ads would be seen by mobile users within a few hundred feet as they tried to log onto the network. It's worthwhile to note that around 75 percent of mobile ads were delivered via Wi-Fi networks.

Then there were real-time exchanges for mobile app publishers—such as MoPub and Nexage—who were rethinking mobile app monetization by enabling publishers to understand ad performance and user engagement. Mobile ad exchanges—unlike mobile ad networks which aggregated advertising inventory and matched it with advertisers, much like online ad networks did—automated many parts of the mobile ad process while connecting publishers with multiple ad networks. MoPub was founded in 2010 by ex-Google and ex-AdMob engineers and product managers who understood the pain points faced by mobile app developers. MoPub's ad serving platform carved out a new way for app publishers to streamline their inventory for advertisers by creating a private marketplace limited to select publishers and advertisers.

In September 2013, Twitter spent US$350 to acquire the world's largest mobile ad exchange. Though MoPub would continue to serve a diverse group of clients—not just Twitter—the acquisition effectively put Twitter in the same elite league as firms like Facebook and Google. While Twitter's own mobile ad credentials will be explained in the next chapter, the MoPub purchase had already put the social network at the forefront of the race to combine effective targeting and mobile ad-buying. Twitter, for instance, could use MoPub's technology to build real-time bidding into its ads platform so advertisers could more easily automate and scale their ads. The combined interest graph could allow Twitter to target ads better than just about anyone else. Twitter, for example, could merge the cookie information from desktop browser and mobile device ID from MoPub to better target specific ad messages.

# A MEANINGFUL BUSINESS

The cost-per-click rates on smartphones were generally higher than what they were for desktop ads. But these mobile ads were geographically targeted to specific set of people in specific demographics, so smartphones could bring higher click rates than advertising to people in general. Tailoring content to specific sets of people rather than the population at large through mobile ads could prove a powerful phenomenon and over the years could change the media landscape. There was clear evidence that consumers were gradually changing the way they shopped, thanks in large part to the apps that reshaped the discovery process with more tempting online offers, easier ways to compare prices, and innovative solutions for attracting customers to stores. Moreover, with location-based apps, retailers were always watching mobile users.

Smartphones, the industry's biggest user growth engine in 2010s, hadn't been well served by advertisers in the early going. Marketers had been initially slow to buy mobile ads, largely because consumers were not visiting mobile websites in large numbers and the process of creating mobile ad campaigns was technically and logistically challenging. Mobile advertising was still untested on a large scale and the business model was in an early stage of development. But now that mobile had presented itself as one of the strongest opportunities in business history, monetizing mobile had become a key agenda item. Once the platforms like iAd and AdMob kick-started this nascent market, marketing pros started paying attention to mobile advertising. The increasing commoditization in wireless handsets and networks also made it imperative that ads become more important as a source of revenue.

Despite the challenges, there was evidence that mobile advertising was becoming a meaningful business, and in some cases a bigger business than online advertising. In fact, it was reminiscent of the Internet in the mid-1990s. People weren't interested in ads and ad fees were low, but advertisers didn't have a choice. They had got to go where audiences were. Mobile advertising could be a bonanza, similar to online advertising a decade ago, but it had been a bit slow off the ground and its growth trajectory was not clear cut. Many brands were just experimenting with mobile and were spending a very small percentage of their ad budget in this space. According to Millennial Media, the sectors that initially spent the most on mobile advertising were telecommunications, retail and restaurants, automotive, finance, and education.

The mobile advertising market grew from US$1.4 billion in 2011 to US$4.1 billion in 2012, and it was projected to hit a massive US$7.3 billion in 2013. And almost all of it was spent on Apple's iOS ecosystem. It's worth noting that, despite all the setbacks outlined in the previous sections, the iPhone platform still came out on top with an average effective cost per thousand impressions (eCPM) of US$2.85 followed by Android devices at US$2.10.Apple's iOS platform drove the highest eCPMs on its network and continued to dominate when it came to monetizing mobile ads. The iPhone's better usability and powerful features allowed more interaction between the advertisement and the device, which in turn, offered better monetization potential than its less user-friendly counterparts.

Advertisers continued to rely heavily on iOS devicesto get their ads in front of mobile users despite the fact that Android was the most widely used mobile operating system. Rich media was another key differentiator in driving engagement and Apple's ad platform demonstrated a clear sway when it came to rich media ad impressions. Moreover, iTunes had a long and successful history of commercial transactions, so people felt comfortable clicking, shopping, and buying on iOS platform. The device itself also counted a lot in relevance to mobile advertisers. Case in point: the iPhone 4S became the top device in mobile ad impressions within a few months of its launch. The iPhone 5 was reckoned to be adopted for mobile ads even more quickly than the 4S.

The other crucial element rapidly gaining clout in the mobile ad anatomy was social media. Mobile-centric social commerce was quickly becoming a new engagement channel. The following chapter digs deeper into how mobile-centric social networking was transforming the mobile commerce landscape.

# 10 THE RISE OF SOCIAL COMMERCE

*"We are a mobile-first advertising company now."*

— Gokul Rajaram, Facebook's product
director for ads

Just about every major digital player had been trying to figure out the mobile revenue dilemma. Facebook, at one stage, admitted that while it owned almost half a billion users on mobile devices, it still wasn't sure whether its mobile business was working or not. Even Google, the world's largest seller of digital ads, couldn't make much of a difference. Suddenly, in summer 2012, one company emerged successful in cracking the mobile ad code. Twitter reported that its mobile advertising business earned more revenue than its website, a surprise given the fact that the company had only been offering mobile ads since early 2012. However, the fact that Twitter got the majority of its usage on mobile immediately solved the mystery. About 60 percent of its 140 million users accessed Twitter on mobile devices as of summer 2012. Furthermore, Twitter's advertising—text and links—seemed ideally suited to the mobile platform.

Twitter ads were integrated into user news feeds in the form of promoted tweets, promoted trends, and hashtags paid for by advertisers. A promoted tweet, for instance, allowed advertisers to engage beyond their core followership and reach more of their target audience. The best part about a tweet promotion was that advertisers had flexibility in their tweet's call to action. They could choose to include the URL of a landing page on their website or include an invitation to their upcoming event. Twitter was able to cash in quietly when everyone else flailed around and tried to find a way to make mobile ads work.

Could Twitter, as a mobile advertising medium, be fundamentally superior to Google or Facebook? Twitter's service was arguably far more efficient as a mobile content-consumption platform; large numbers of people saw it as a mobile information network with real-time content about interesting topics—both news- and entertainment-related. The micro-blogging service also had the potential to be better at targeting around specific events or locations than either Google or Facebook, which could give it an edge as the market grew.

Twitter could build a great mobile ad business on two key merits. First, Twitter was inherently a mobile-first product. Twitter ads appeared to be more effective on mobile than they were on the desktop. Second, unlike other forms of digital advertising, Twitter ads were same on the mobile and the desktop. It was crucial because mobile ads, particularly display ads, didn't have the same performance on mobile as they did on the desktop. Twitter ads' similarity across desktop and mobile platforms also made life easier for advertisers since they could have the same creative work and format for mobile and desktop campaigns.

An equally thrilling development was Twitter's partnership with American Express, which allowed people to buy things by tweeting. An American Express customer synched her credit card to her Twitter account and started making purchases by putting hashtags in her tweets that corresponded with special deals American Express was offering. She sent a tweet to her followers about that particular item and included the hashtag. American Express sent her a confirmation tweet and the transaction was complete. Twitter didn't get a cut of the American Express purchases. Though the program appeared to have broken new ground, American Express wasn't the first company to see potential in Twitter-based commerce or "t-commerce." In 2012, a startup called Chirpify had linked up with PayPal to let users buy and sell things on Twitter using @ handles.

Though Twitter had been initially seen as a form of communication, the prologue of this book has attempted to establish the common heritage through the work of Jack Dorsey, the co-founder of both Twitter and Square. Now the partnership between American Express and Twitter was a testament of a larger push by social networks into commerce. Social networks took all the information they had about users and tried to make money off it. In Twitter's case, that meant taking the web of relationships people had built on the network and using it to push products. The fact that Twitter didn't have the best reputation for security, and that Twitter accounts were notoriously hackable, didn't bother American Express. First, Twitter never got the credit-card information; it stayed with American Express. Second, in addition to the confirmation tweet, American Express sent a confirmation e-mail when a transaction went through, so if someone did hijack a customer's Twitter account and ran up a tab, the customer would know right away.

Why had the social media stalwart finally turned its attention toward mobile commerce? A mobile device was the most personal tool a user constantly accessed, so it didn't surprise many when the social media segment grew to represent the majority of a consumer's mobile usage. Almost half of traffic on Facebook and Twitter was mobile by 2012. The mobile-only audience was growing faster than the multichannel or desktop-only audience and the mobile-only audience would most likely dominate the social network in the long-term. That's why social media icons like Facebook and Twitter were in a big hurry to figure out mobile. Moreover, social networks were becoming a great form of discovery. So the mobile ads bandwagon was going to have huge ramifications for social media players like Facebook, Twitter and Pandora whose audiences were rapidly shifting to mobile devices. Another hot button: many people in the industry saw promise in ventures like Foursquare and Instagram because they believed that these upstarts could reinvent social from scratch for a mobile device.

# FACEBOOK A MOBILE COMPANY

Meanwhile, Facebook was under the gun to show it could make money from 600 million users accessing the social network through mobile, especially during the Facebook's initial public offering (IPO) fiasco when analysts raised the issues related to company's failure to monetize on the mobile side. Just before its highly anticipated IPO in May 2012, Facebook revealed that it wasn't making any significant revenue from its mobile website or app—even though more than half its 900 million members used the service on mobile devices. That made Facebook the poster child for Internet companies blindsided by the rapid shift of online activity from desktop to smartphones and tablets. There was a huge question mark if Facebook would ever figure out how to really make money off the hundreds of millions of people that used its mobile platform.

It was about time for Facebook to focus on mobile. Gaining traction in mobile advertising was critical for Facebook; 60 percent of its users logged in from mobile phones. According to a comScore report, Facebook users spent 441 minutes a month on Facebook mobile. Facebook had an unbelievable amount of knowledge on its individual users. If Facebook combined its individual user knowledge with mobile search and commerce, its mobile advertising could become something really valuable. It could, for instance, power brand recommendations and strategically geo-target them. But Facebook confronted all the usual problems: small screens, fewer technologies to target potential customers, and gaps in marketers' ability to measure the impact of mobile ads.

For a start, making the transition to the small screen had been a challenge: most Facebook ads appeared on the right side of the web page, so there was nowhere to show them on a mobile device. However, there were several different types of advertising products that Facebook could implement in mobile. The easiest would likely be interstitial and banner ads within Facebook's native apps and mobile website presence, but creating effective ads for screens smaller than five inches had proved problematic not just for Facebook, but for almost every other mobile ad network as well. Facebook could also capitalize on the "interest graph" it had created through its social graph platform. This was essentially what Facebook was doing on its desktop platform—targeting ads to people based on their interests. But again, optimizing screen real-estate and not alienating mobile users would be the hardest part for Facebook.

At that time, Facebook's advertising team was too preoccupied evangelizing a new kind of desktop ad—sponsored stories—to pay much attention to mobile. These ads were based on actions by a Facebook member, such as "liking" a page or checking in at a store, which marketers could then promote, for a fee, to the member's friends. By early 2012, Facebook was ready to start running them not just in the right-hand section reserved for ads but also on its prime real estate: the news feed, where people spent most of their time on the social network. Executives knew it was a risky step into the unknown—especially when they extended the same type of ads to mobile as well. Sponsored stories got more clicks but it was the mobile versions that really took off. They got twice as many clicks and commanded nearly triple the price from advertisers as those on the desktop, according to a study by advertising agency TBG Digital.

Facebook had finally answered the mobile call by making several changes to its self-serve ad model. The Menlo Park, California–based company started allowing sponsored stories in users' mobile news feeds. These ads were targeted by items users had "liked." That eventually led to a new advertising model in which ads would be targeted based on the apps a mobile user had on his phone and didn't consider whether a user had indicated an interest in a subject. The ads would appear on mobile devices in Facebook's news feed, a stream of updates from friends on the home page. By July 2012, the mobile ads were grossing US$500,000 a day. To push in-store shopping during Thanksgiving weekend, Walmart bought 50 million mobile ads from Facebook, rivaling the reach of TV campaigns. Facebook didn't launch its first mobile-only advertising product until June 2012. Since then, it had built one of the biggest mobile advertising businesses in the world.

What Facebook discovered was that integrating ads directly into a user's flow of natural activities worked far better than banners and pop-up ads. While these so-called native ads, which mixed marketing into content, might be controversial, they looked like advertising's most successful adaptation yet to mobile computing. A lot of industry watchers, even Zuckerberg, worried that users might balk at ads mixed with posts from friends. By and large, that didn't happen. A Facebook study found that the insertion of ads reduced comments, likes, and other interaction with news feed updates by 2 percent, a small decline that the company deemed acceptable.

Facebook launched another mobile ad product in the fall 2012 that allowed makers of mobile apps to urge users to install their games or programs. Facebook would give developers and advertisers the ability to place ads for mobile apps in a user's news feed and charge advertisers each time a user downloaded the advertised app. It was the first ad in the mobile news feed that didn't require advertisers to wait for a "like" or other social action to create it. Advertisers instead could use Facebook's trove of biographical data from user profiles to target likely prospects, as they were accustomed to doing with traditional ads. Take Cie Games which used app installation ads to attract players for its first iPhone game, Car Town Streets. Cie Games found out that the cost of acquiring users was 40 percent lower using Facebook's ads than those from other mobile ad networks, and these users spent more inside the game.

The social giant tracked the apps that people used through its popular Facebook Connect feature, which let users log into millions of websites and apps as varied as Amazon.com, LinkedIn and Yelp with their Facebook identity. Facebook then targeted ads based on that data. By doing so, Facebook went a step further than mobile-ad networks, which tracked what ads people had clicked on through a phone's web browser. For instance, if someone was a frequent player of social game maker Zynga's "Words with Friends" game, ads for other Zynga games would then show up in that mobile user's news feed. It was in a stark contrast to Apple whose privacy policy dictated that it couldn't target ads based on apps a person had downloaded from its App Store and iTunes. Google also didn't target ads based on similar data, though in theory it could. So these networks weren't aware of all the apps that a user had on his phone.

In 2012, Facebook brought in more mobile ad revenue than any other company besides Google. Shortly afterward, in

January 2013, Zuckerberg described Facebook as a "mobile company."Facebook's success had exploded some myths of mobile marketing. Advertisers often complained that they couldn't run big, flashy ads on tiny screens. But Facebook's mobile ads took up a larger part of the screen than ads aimed at desktop computers typically would—one reason they got so many clicks. Some mobile ads even included photos; next, Facebook was actively looking at incorporating video into them.

Hundreds of millions of Internet users entrusted their online identity to Facebook and now the company was taking that model from desktop to the mobile world. For years Facebook pushed the boundaries of privacy and sharing, and with time, many of those product decisions, such as the news feed and check-ins, ended up being accepted or even enjoyed. Now the iconic social network was experimenting to see if it could push those same boundaries to benefit businesses, not just users' connection to their friends. While this mobile ad platform offered new possibilities for Facebook to monetize, it was imperative that the social behemoth remained transparent about it and provided ways for users to opt-out of the mobile ad targeting if they wanted.

## NEW INFLECTION POINTS

It was now social networks at large that looked to mobile commerce to remain relevant and successful. In May 2012, just when Facebook launched its IPO, the company acquired mobile commerce startup Karma, which made apps for gifting friends and family. The deal was Facebook's second-largest acquisition to date, but unlike past acquisitions, where Facebook bought small companies mostly for their talented engineers, the social networking giant planned to continue running Karma's service and regarded the purchase as an important step in its thrust into the m-commerce business. Not only was it Facebook's first major step into e-commerce—the social networking company had so far dabbled in payments through virtual goods and social games—it gave Facebook users another reason to use the platform from their mobile devices. It was also harbinger of the fact that Facebook could eventually allow users to purchase within its platform to generate transactional revenue.

Karma, which bought items from manufacturers and sold them for a profit, gave Facebook a new business line and a new entry point into the transactions business. The individual retailers handled all the shipping, while Facebook's payments platform—the same one used for Facebook Games—handled the money-changing part. Once a user loaded the app on a smartphone, Karma connected with Facebook and gleaned data from the social network to know when friends' birthdays, graduations, weddings, and other life events would occur. Karma then suggested gifts to the user from its curated catalog, and once a purchase was made, the lucky friend received a message requesting his or her physical address and, in some cases, offering the option to customize the gift, like changing the color or choosing to donate the money instead. The social-gifting app helped consumers remember to buy a gift and discover products without having to wander through a department store.

The biggest challenge for Facebook was to generate revenue streams in the mobile space because, as of 2012, wireless advertising was not living up to expectations. The purchase would help Facebook build up monetization prowess on mobile platforms and produce new revenue streams from its mobile app. In a matter of weeks, Facebook also unveiled its App Center which would act as a central repository for apps tied to its social platform. Monetizing mobile was a billion-dollar opportunity for the social behemoth and allowing users to get personalized app recommendations on their phones through the Facebook app could prove pivotal for that goal. There were other distinct avenues the company could take to make money from mobile: direct and indirect ad placement and payment platforms like Facebook Credits.

However, in summer 2012, Facebook ended its three-year experiment with the virtual currency, Credits. Now users would simply have a Facebook account with a balance measured in U.S. dollars in the United States or whatever currency was native to a country. But why did Facebook phase out Credits which earned it 15 percent of 2011 revenue from payments primarily from social games? Payment as a revenue source was too important to Facebook's future to take the risk of promoting an untested and unproven virtual currency. Moreover, to establish Credits, Facebook would have to spend significant amount of resources in educating the public and building the brand of Credits. It was a much easier solution to simply transact in an already established currency that users understand and utilize. But more crucially, Facebook was aiming to build a platform where consumers were comfortable buying the products and applications they found valuable, and where developers and innovators could generate significant revenue by selling the products they were building.

Facebook was now in the process of building out its mobile app ecosystem that included the Facebook App Center and an easy-to-implement and easy-to-use payment system. A simple payment system was the first step in supporting the App Center. In fact, a central application repository and a way to pay for those apps were basic ingredients when creating a flourishing apps ecosystem. Facebook's new member accounts would function similarly to an iTunes account: a user added a credit card to her account, digital goods could be purchased and immediately charged to the card on file, or could be drawn from stored value in that account. If a user was given a Facebook gift card—in card or digital form—she would add that reward code to her account and that value would be stored until she used it. Next up, the social web giant partnered with mobile operators in thirty countries to create a direct-to-carrier billing system for mobile web apps available through Facebook.

The new payment system, while showing Facebook's efforts to make it easier for in-app purchases, also hinted on the social media firm's broader strategy: make money off mobile beyond advertisements and banner displays. Search, discovery, customer services, rankings, and other support structures could come in due time. The social media behemoth, for instance, could effectively create hyper-local services to benefit both users and local advertisers. Facebook's user base comprised nearly a fifth of the earth's population, and the company had all of the data needed to ensure that there was activity wherever the service was offered from day one.

With around a billion users, the scale of Facebook's reach was simply staggering. In fact, Facebook had become the world's largest directory of individuals and local businesses.

One of the most alluring prospects for Facebook could be in location-aware push notifications. Facebook had already started adding location to users' posts on both desktop and mobile platforms and the acquisition of ambient social location startup Glancee could further boost the company's association with location technology. Glancee knew where a mobile user was, ran in the background of mobile service, and told the user when a friend of his was nearby. Facebook could use Glancee's technology to connect not just people to people, but also people to stores, merchants, and restaurants. The social behemoth could create location-aware push notification based on users' interest graph, add incentives like coupons and deals to lure users to businesses, and cut a deal for itself. Such motives were also complemented by the widespread perception about Facebook eventually launching its own smartphone: it's best to control the hardware if there is difficulty in securing margins from ads placed by others.

Then there was the January 2011 acquisition of Rel8tion which specialized in hyper-local ad targeting. The asset could be merged with the Facebook Exchange real-time ad bidding system to create a powerful new product for advertisers. When a user opened a mobile app while granting Facebook the permission to pull in GPS coordinates or when a user published a location-tagged post, Facebook would learn his location and assume he would be nearby for the next few minutes. Advertisers would pre-submit ads to be shown to users in specific locations, and possibly a maximum bid they would pay to have their ad shown. When a user was in one of these areas, Facebook would match mobile users with advertisers and either automatically serve the highest-bid as a pre-made hyper-local ad, or ask a demand-side platform hired by the advertiser to make a bid and then show the ad of the auction's winner.

Facebook's real-time hyper-local advertising could allow local businesses to advertise to people in sight of their brick-and-mortar store, or let travel companies target people when they were away from their home city. For instance, Best Buy electronics chain could set up ads targeted to people within 1,000 feet of all its retail locations in the United States who "liked" Best Buy, other electronics stores, or devices it sold. When a mobile user opened his Facebook app while walking or driving nearby, he would see in his news feed a mobile sponsored story about how his friend had interacted with Best Buy, or possibly an offer for a discount from Best Buy that could make him more likely to visit the physical store. Some users might not be entirely comfortable with such hyper-local targeting, but Facebook would likely stress that all data was anonymized and no business would know their personal location.

Next up, Facebook, knowing so much about everyone's location and preferences, could define specific "neighborhood" in a number of dimensions and affinities, such as distance, shared interests, political affiliation, and so on. A neighborhood feed would become an ambient stream about what was happening near a mobile user, as well as a way to passively discover new people, places and events. It would become a veritable neighborhood newspaper and online forum of sorts, a perfect place to run ads, which could be precisely targeted by neighborhood, user demographics, and even time of day. All this could transform Facebook into a utility and a community-level communications powerhouse. While social networks for neighborhoods existed, they didn't thrive because they had a hard time recruiting users at scale.

## INSTAGRAM CAPTURED

Facebook's foray into the multi-faceted m-commerce world didn't end here. The firm that finally proved that display advertising could work for mobile—Instagram—had also been bought for a staggering US$1 billion by Facebook in 2012. It was one of the biggest acquisitions in the Web 2.0 world, especially for a generation of startups which grew up in the post-iPhone app world. Initially, Facebook's purchase of the Instagram was seen as a defensive move to keep Instagram out of Twitter's hands. The emergence of Instagram as a mobile-only social platform had set off "photo wars" and suddenly the app was pulled into an acquisition race among the industry stalwarts like Apple, Facebook, Tumbler, and Twitter. Instagram—before pivoting into photo sharing and growing into a juggernaut—began in 2010 as a startup called Burbn that attempted to compete with Foursquare.

Kevin Systrom and Mike Krieger were able to eventually turn this scrappy startup into a platform for mobile users that was meant to be a play; they could capture the world and parcel it back to friends who were out there doing just the same. Instagram's approximately 39 million users—according to AppData's early 2013 statistics—not only looked at mobile ads; they rated them, shared them, and commented on them. They were not being seen as ads though, but rather as pictures. However, they could help brands appear more favorable in a way that glossy magazine pictures couldn't, because they were not the commoditized images that consumers were used to see. For instance, behind-the-scenes shots of models and fashion shoots! A number of celebrities were already using their large followings on Instagram for brand endorsements.

Facebook's tweak of Instagram's terms of service was widely seen as an indication of social media behemoth's groundwork to monetize the photo-sharing app; the changes could pave the way to allow advertisers to buy space in Instagram users' photo streams. They could also allow Instagram to use Facebook's data to personalize the Instagram user experience and perhaps target ads. Facebook was building up its service as an advertising network and Instagram was evidently a crucial part in its monetization and advertising ambitions. Emily White—Sheryl Sandberg's protégé at both Google and Facebook—had worked on AdWords and later on Facebook's mobile partnerships; her choice to lead Instagram's team seemed a harbinger of the fact that mobile ads would eventually start to appear in the Instagram feed.

By autumn 2013, Instagram had more than 150 million active users a month, a gain of roughly 128 million since Facebook bought the app. White was charged with turning this billion-dollar acquisition that had never made money into a real business. And the challenge was to figure out how to integrate advertising without jeopardizing Instagram's cool factor.

# 11 E-COMMERCE UNTETHERED

> *"When Rupert [Murdoch] invades your privacy...
> it's against the law. When Mark [Zuckerberg]
> does, it's the future."*

> — Bill Keller, former executive editor,
> *The New York Times*

The U.S. retail chain Best Buy lost business during the 2011 Christmas shopping season when people standing in its stores took mobile reads of barcodes and found items priced more cheaply on Amazon.com. Some customers even ordered while they were still on the retailer's property. The smartphone disruption had reached the doorstep of retail stores and had demonstrated the power to change commerce significantly. The rich smartphone experience had earlier rendered devices like PDA, payphone, personal navigation device, and digital still camera largely irrelevant. A harbinger of things to come in the brick-and-mortar space: the limited kiosk presence within large stores looked in danger of being disrupted by a far more dynamic and connected environment where people could shop online in real-time using their handheld devices. The promise of mobile commerce had finally come of age.

Society witnessed the democratization of information during the mid- to late 1990's period when companies like Google and Yahoo! made data available to everyone regardless of where or who they were. After that came the democratization of information distribution with services like Facebook and Twitter, allowing anyone to broadcast their content and potentially attract an audience. Concurrently, the democratization of computing power occurred on the smartphone platform with billions of people in the world gaining access to computers because of the availability of low-cost mobile devices. Smartphones provided seamless and slick connections over Wi-Fi and 3/4G networks. These devices, equipped with extremely powerful and efficient processors, ran on advanced and feature-rich operating system platforms like Android and iOS to enable highly innovative new applications.

So what was up next? Many in the industry thought of the world of buying and selling. These observers saw a new era around the democratization of commerce. In the past, companies like Walmart rose to the top of the commerce value chain by simply being the best at aggregating a suite of products into a large, single space. These large outfits mastered the art of mass aggregation and built up their own brand names to make shoppers feel secure in buying things from them. Now this mass aggregation was at risk of disruption at the hands of a new commerce technology. Small upstarts like Square had become the icons of this democratization for both buyers and sellers. Mobile commerce—buying and selling of goods through mobile devices—was now perceived as the next chapter of the e-commerce playbook and was on a dramatically steep rise. People could do almost everything on an always-on mobile device that evolved with the constant interactivity of the Internet.

Many industry watchers viewed m-commerce as a strategic part of the larger e-commerce world. There was a huge overlap between the e-commerce and m-commerce domains: for instance, areas like online payment and shopping. But the contrasting worlds of smartphone and PC dictated that a lot of things that a user could do on a personal computer were not practical on a smartphone due to its smaller screen. At the same time, however, there were opportunities that went beyond e-commerce because m-commerce applications utilized the unique characteristics of the mobile realm. First, the anywhere aspect of mobile provided ubiquitous and instant access to commerce applications such as POS interaction and stock market transactions. A mobile user on the street could instantly respond to a marketing campaign through a QR code. Second, the local aspect of mobile facilitated context and location-aware services in the form of coupons, deals, and loyalty rewards. Third, the social facet of the mobile world helped spread recommendations and other forms of viral marketing. Fourth, the personal characteristics of mobile enabled targeted marketing based on collected user behavior patterns.

The marriage of computing and connectivity without the shackles of being tethered to a location was one of the biggest disruptive forces of the twenty-first century IT juggernaut. Mobile commerce was a living example. The e-commerce world essentially provided the visual experience of buying goods and services online. Now the same wealth of information and the same degree of control were being taken from the home desktop to a mobile setting for people, for instance, waiting in the check-out line at a store. Mobile commerce provided consumers with greater flexibility while giving merchants the opportunity to provide individualized offers and rewards in real-time.

This book has explored all the major building blocks of the m-commerce juggernaut—location services, mobile payments, and wireless ads. But if there was one single phenomenon that was central to all of these vital signs of m-commerce, it was security. Concerns about security and privacy wouldn't stall the m-commerce thrust because the smartphone revolution was irreversible and m-commerce apps were an intrinsic part of the smartphone bandwagon. On the flip side, however, despite the astronomical growth of smartphones and tablets, and the rise of apps allowing consumers to purchase both virtual and real goods from their mobile devices, m-commerce hadn't taken off to the degree many expected. According to some experts, one of the major reasons for this lag was that mobile authentication methods had not caught up to the level of innovation seen in mobile hardware and applications development.

## NEW SECURITY PARADIGM

Typing strong passwords for authentication was a cumbersome task even on desktops where consumers carried dozens of passwords and PINs, each consisting of a series of uppercase and lowercase letters, numbers and symbols. This traditional approach to authentication was nearly impossible to replicate on mobile devices as users struggled to enter their clunky passwords on relatively tiny, soft keypads. Smartphone users generally struggled with mobile transactions because of login troubles, and consequently, negative experiences caused them to abandon m-commerce transactions. Likewise, security and fraud concerns were slowing consumer adoption of mobile commerce and mobile banking initiatives. Mobile users were generally wary of linking their credit card data and other financial information to apps on smartphones because the device could be easily lost or stolen. Moreover, keystroke-logging malware and phishing attacks targeting smartphone and tablet users were proliferating rapidly, with the goal of capturing passwords, PINs, and other account information.

In a *Forbes* guest post titled "Mobile Commerce Needs New Authentication Schemes," Curtis Staker, CEO of Confident Technologies, argued that if consumers didn't trust that the mobile apps or the smart devices themselves were secure, m-commerce would continue to be stunted. The authentication process was often a security aspect most visible to users and it directly influenced consumers' perception of trust. For mobile commerce to grow, businesses would have to stop relying on archaic, password-based security processes that inconvenienced customers and provided a poor level of protection. People generally chose weak passwords and used the same password for multiple online accounts and applications. Fraudsters—who used keystroke-logging malware to capture usernames, passwords, and PINs—knew that if they captured one password, they could gain access to a number of accounts. And because the vast majority of users didn't install security software on their smartphones or tablets, it was easy for fraudsters to plant keyloggers and other malware simply by tricking people into clicking on an untrustworthy link.

Therefore, mobile companies, instead of relying on a static password of the user's choice, needed to incorporate authentication technologies that generated one-time passwords for their websites and apps. By creating a unique password or authentication code every time, new security mechanisms in the mobile realm could eliminate many of the most common problems that had haunted the desktop online world. Facebook, for example, had raised the mobile security bar when it launched Code Generator as a social authentication tool. Code Generator—integrated into Facebook's Login Approvals feature for confirming logins made on new devices—enabled users to more easily confirm logins via mobile devices.

Staker noted in his article that smartphones and tablets had unique characteristics—including touchscreens, microphones, and gyroscopes—that made it possible to utilize advanced authentication techniques otherwise not possible in the past on traditional PCs. The building blocks in smartphones and tablets, including touchscreens and sensors, made it possible for users to securely authenticate mobile transactions with just a few taps on the screen. So instead of forcing mobile users to type complex passwords on tiny keypads, the mobile industry could look to new authentication techniques that were designed to take advantage of the graphical touchscreen displays of smartphones and tablets. Pattern- and image-based authentication techniques delivered a more natural and intuitive way for users to authenticate. Rather than remembering another arbitrary string of letters, numbers and symbols, such authentication methods could ask the user to draw a pattern on the screen, touch a series of points on a picture, or tap pictures to identify which ones matched their secret authentication categories. Some image-based authentication techniques, for instance, generated one-time passwords.

Sensors were becoming a ubiquitous feature on smartphones, which in turn, made biometrics and pattern-recognition viable authentication methods. Microphones could be used for voice recognition; cameras could be employed for facial recognition; and even behaviors such as the rhythm and pace with which the person walked could be sensed by the smartphone's gyroscope and accelerometer as ways to authenticate a person. Apple's launch of Siri on the iPhone platform was setting the stage for innovative voice recognition capabilities. For high-value transactions, biometrics could be used to authenticate a person or ensure that it was the legitimate owner of the smartphone or tablet conducting the transaction and not another person who might have stolen the device. The image-based authentication approaches were also faster for mobile users to execute, allowing mobile shoppers to quickly complete their purchases with minimal friction or stumbling blocks that could otherwise cause them to abandon the transaction. Android's Ice Cream Sandwich version provided a stepping stone for such applications by utilizing facial recognition technology to unlock a user's phone.

In August 2013, Motorola's first Google-era phone—the Moto X—raised the ante by introducing touchless voice controls that could be used to create voice recognition-based authentication. A month later, Apple incorporated a fingerprint scanner into the iPhone 5S' home button to enable biometric security for mobile commerce-like apps. The era of one-tap authentication had kick-started with the launch of Apple's Touch ID feature. Consumers also needed to be assured that if they lost their phone or it got stolen, their financial information would be secure. Taking steps like encrypting credit card data directly on the device as soon as the user entered it or implementing one-click check-out so that the user wouldn't need to enter credit card data on the device again helped to ensure that if a mobile device was lost or stolen, a fraudster couldn't gain access to the credit card data.

The long-term success of m-commerce hinged on assuring consumers that their information was in safe hands. By 2012, consumer expectations in regards to security and privacy issues had largely shifted because they lived their lives more online than ever before. Consumers now seemed willing to accept a certain degree of loss of privacy in the digital age and this shift in consumer attitude could largely be attributed to Facebook. The Facebook success story and privacy options the company provided showed this stark reality that consumers just wanted more control and that giving consumers choices didn't necessarily mean they were going to opt out. Consumers wanted to enjoy greater trust while conducting m-commerce transactions which otherwise boasted a number of upsides. For instance, the m-commerce information stream was highly encrypted and was safer than credit cards placed in the consumer's physical wallet.

Mobile banking was steadily making headway despite the fact that perceived security risks remained a hindrance to full adoption of the technology. In mobile banking, for instance, consumers could mitigate fraud in real-time: SMS and push messages for mobile devices allowed consumers to help banks monitor fraudulent transactions as they happened. Furthermore, unlike credit card information, which was broadcast and unencrypted, mobile wallet communications was a two-way handshake between consumer and retailer. If a mobile user lost his phone, he could remotely scrub all the data; but if he lost his wallet, he wouldn't know where the cards were. Data analytics could also play a crucial role in helping spot fraud trends. Going forward, security technology in the m-commerce era was likely to become highly automated through more sophisticated tools and greater security awareness.

## SMALLER BITS LARGER VISION

In retrospect, this all looked similar to the early days of e-commerce in the mid-1990s. Back then, the first phase of the e-commerce world was all about pure play—Internet users bought things online and got them shipped to their house. Now, just the way the launch of the Netscape browser had laid the foundation for the e-commerce bonanza, the advent of the iPhone helped people become accustomed to m-commerce options like buying apps, games and songs on their mobile handsets. A brand new experience for smartphone users brought a plethora of new technologies to the m-commerce bandwagon and began to transform the creative confusion into clarity of a larger vision.

There was, for instance, the cloud factor. All payment and loyalty information interchange could eventually happen over the cloud. The services that complemented mobile commerce—rich location storage, social integration, push notifications, check-ins, status updates, and device identification—could all be carried out more effectively from the cloud. The cloud-based m-commerce architecture offered the inherent benefit of organizing identification, payment, marketing, and ads into a single compelling product. As per tradition in the technology world, startup companies were among the first to warm up to this tech hot spot. Identive Group offered a cloud-based NFC tag management platform, which allowed advertisers, retailers and organizations in the education, hospitality and other industries to manage the delivery of targeted content and services on NFC-enabled mobile devices. Another upstart Lemon.com offered a handy cloud-based receipt organizer and spending tracker mobile app. The PIN-protected app—working mainly as a backup for safe-keeping of physical credit cards, store and loyalty cards, ID cards, insurance cards, and more—subsequently expanded into a platform to include mobile wallet functionality.

The digital hub was clearly moving to the cloud, and m-commerce apps were a crucial part of this shift given the security, storage efficiency, and content richness that the cloud promised to bring to m-commerce services. Take the case of

NCR Corp.—the Duluth, Georgia–based maker of cash registers and ATM machines—which set to launch a cloud-based POS service aimed at small businesses. The billion dollar company was pinning hopes to make an entry into the seemingly lucrative payment pie with its history of strength in handling secure payments and experience in providing back-end support. Another testament of the cloud power: the e-commerce pioneer Groupon grew up extremely fast thanks in large part to cloud computing. It started on Amazon's cloud services and moved to its own data centers as late as 2012. The strategy allowed Groupon to do more with less IT people.

In businesses where the sales force predominantly relied on telephone calls, face-to-face meetings, and printed marketing brochures, m-commerce apps using the power of cloud could herald a new era of automation-centric efficiency. Sales people, for example, could access digital marketing material along with customer profiles and preferences, and they could track everything that customer needed to know about the product during a sales call. Moreover, they could track special incentives, overdue payments, and all such information while still on the road. A travel agent, for instance, could facilitate booking and ticket arrangements, provide alerts about canceled flights, and offer plans for alternate arrangements all via a smartphone tied to the cloud.

There were other enabling technologies that could attract people to the right places and thus could boost m-commerce industry by refining mobile advertising as well as location-centric shopping. Google's Project Glass using augmented reality goggles was one such amalgam of innovative new technologies that not only promised to define the next-generation smartphone, but also took m-commerce initiatives to a whole new level. The project masterfully mixed video communications with the latest developments in augmented reality, navigation, and location apps to let the goggles user know where he was standing, inquired where he wanted to go, like a certain floor in a mall, and worked out a route to take him there. While the user wandered around a certain neighborhood, the app collected whatever information it could capture from GPS signals, public Wi-Fi transmitters, and cellular towers.

A user of Google goggles, for instance, while checking her e-mail, could notice that the sushi place across the street was offering 40 percent discount on her favorite dish. She could place an order with a little bit of tilting and nodding, and by the time she crossed the street, the dish would be ready for takeout. While apps like Google Glass conveniently pointed mobile users to a restaurant, a convenience store or a tourist attraction, they in fact prompted them to explore new areas with an alluring sense of social discovery. Augmented reality apps were evidently directing smartphones and tablets to a powerful new world of discovery. Augmented reality technology could take off on commercial scale once wearable systems like Google Glass became popular and the mobile industry found a way to monetize the value that came with such discovery applications.

In a move to counter Google, archrival Apple launched a free, voice-enabled GPS navigation app onto the iPhone platform. The Maps service also included real-time traffic, Yelp integration, crowd-sourced traffic data, and Siri support. On top of that, Apple planned to add three-dimensional modeling for buildings and terrain data. The mobile industry was apparently looking to leverage location information, gestures, and user-interface advancements to reduce complexity and provide far more compelling services. The m-commerce proposition could benefit from this combination of GPS, open-graph technologies, and the social web to create services that were not plausible before.

Another m-commerce bright spot: smartphone users were increasingly doing online browsing on their handsets. Much of the content in this book in relation to m-commerce initiatives relates to apps—from location to payments to mobile ads. That's because modern m-commerce platforms were intrinsically linked to the smartphone movement where apps were a defining theme. However, as chronicled in chapter 1, mobile websites had an important role to play in the overall development of m-commerce business. Case in point: while retailers pushed mobile users to download dedicated apps, many users were turning more and more to mobile websites. In 2012, mobile users were spending more minutes on apps than mobile websites because native apps were more powerful than mobile websites—but the gap was closing. Ultimately, mobile websites would continue to get better through the maturation of HTML5, which could further narrow the gap between native apps and the mobile web.

Retailers embarking on e-commerce operations were increasingly building mobile-optimized sites because, as opposed to native apps, which worked on specific platforms like Android and iPhone, mobile sites rendered information to all Internet-enabled phones. Take the example of Uber, the cab ordering service which allowed city dwellers to quickly and easily get around through an app on their iPhone or Android devices.

Once the service became popular, the San Francisco–based upstart launched a new mobile website m.uber.com to allow Blackberry and Windows Phone owners to use the service and thus expand the potential user base. Moreover, mobile websites were inherently more suitable for specific user groups like stock market professionals. So, the power of apps aside, developing a mobile-friendly website would still be the foundation stone of a business' mobile game plan.

Mobile Internet was expected to surpass 2 billion users by 2015, thus outpacing desktop web usage. The real opportunity was in converting those browsers—who were growing by the day—into purchasers. If consumers spent more time browsing the web on their mobile devices than traditional devices like desktop PCs, they could ultimately end up shopping and purchasing more on those mobile devices as well. The opportunity clearly existed by making the mobile shopping experience as easy as possible for the consumer. A good mobile shopping experience was the one that was fully optimized for the smaller screen, took advantage of touchscreen technology, and offered a fast check-out in as few steps as possible.

Tablets were also quickly emerging as a bright spot in the "anytime, anywhere" m-commerce playbook. Although there were far fewer tablets in the market than there were smartphones, as of 2013, tablets were already transforming the online shopping landscape. In fact, when it came to the conversion rate of visiting users into actual shoppers and the average amount they spent, tablets were already at parity with PC-based shopping. The iPad contributed to more traffic than any other portable device, taking 10 percent of online shopping. There was no question that the tablet was far more convenient than the smartphone when it came to completing a transaction online. Phone screens were so tiny that browsing products online and entering credit card information was a pain. According to a survey of fifty five online retailers by Forrester, in 2012, tablets accounted for 3.2 percent of all U.S. online retail sales, more than double the 1.5 percent share for smartphones.

# THE M-COMMERCE CHRONICLE

Digital payment systems were not a new concept. Science fiction writers like Arthur C. Clarke and Ray Bradbury had predicted electronic commerce and futuristic payment systems long before they existed. Clarke had envisaged online banking in his work while Bradbury's Guy Montag from "Fahrenheit 451" used an ATM years before it was invented. Fast forward to 2013 and mobile users could check their bank balance, pay for groceries, and give their kids allowance through a small device which they carried around all day. That clearly indicated people's intense desire for a simple, portable and personal way to interact with their finances. Mobile payment platforms explained in chapters 4 and 5 mostly catered to the POS side of the story because of the revolutionary impact of new technologies like NFC and QR codes on the mobile shopping experience.

However, an m-commerce area that needs mention in the concluding part of the book is peer-to-peer or person-to-person mobile payments that involve the direct transfer of funds from one person to another using a mobile device. These bank-grade mobile money services had a crucial role to play in the larger m-commerce world. Zong—which offered a mobile payments platform that let people pay for items online via direct billing to their mobile phone—was acquired by PayPal and later integrated into its larger m-commerce operations. Then there was Boku which allowed mobile phone users to shop online and charge their mobile phone bill through a two-step authorization process. When a user wanted to purchase an item, he could enter his cell phone number on the website. The site sent a text message to the mobile phone, the user confirmed the transaction with a short reply, and all the charges showed up on his phone bill.

Mobile commerce channels like mobile websites and peer-to-peer mobile transactions would most likely evolve over time and make a vital impact on the business scene. The fate of mobile websites to carry out m-commerce transactions was generally tied to the evolution of HTML5. Peer-to-peer mobile transactions, on the other hand, could grow faster in countries like India and Kenya which lacked digital payment infrastructure. In the developing world, it was a question of extending the benefits of participation in the financial system to broader and deeper segments of the population, many of whom didn't have access to mainstream financial services and mostly relied on cash. For example, in 2012, around 88 percent of the Indian population carried mobile phones versus 2 percent penetration of debit and credit cards. So the mobile phone could serve here as a gateway to the financial system.

Apparently, peer-to-peer payments served their distinct needs. The emerging markets like Brazil and India, which hardly had any banks in rural areas, were leapfrogging rich markets by going straight to mobile banking. In these markets, banks were also reaching far beyond their traditional branch networks by using agents, often shopkeepers in small villages, equipped with mobile phones and card readers. Customers could make small deposits, withdrawals, and money transfers through these agents instead of visiting faraway branches. Conversely, the availability of peer-to-peer payment systems in the United States was more of a novelty because money could be switched easily via bank transfers, checks, or other means. Mobile money was sure a play for the emerging middle class in Africa and Asia, but the developed world was at work on how to break the middle-class's credit card habit in an attempt to introduce contactless payments via smartphones.

In fact, even the need for mobile payments—NFC or otherwise—was not as pressing in the United States as it was in other parts of the world. In the United States and some other developed countries, mobile commerce in general, and mobile payments in specific, were not based on critical need but rather on creating extra value for the consumer. Mobile payments' use in developed countries was skewed heavily toward young males mostly because they were cool. In developed markets like the United States, it was about convenience, choice, control, and flexibility in managing money. Mobile commerce business in America seemed to be on a higher plateau because the existing infrastructure was synched to the new initiatives. There were robust carrier billing options, PayPal and other online payment services, as well as retail destinations like Amazon, eBay, and others.

Furthermore, in developed markets like the United States, smartphone makers were keen to maintain feature differentiation and ecosystem lock-in to preserve their margins, and part of this would come through m-commerce features. After 2010, when smartphone and tablet use proliferated, mobile commerce sales also quadrupled. Mobile commerce had been one of those elite technologies which the industry had been talking about for a number of years, and when experts talked about it, they generally said it's just two years away. Then, there came the iPhone juggernaut and m-commerce actually started kicking off. Now, ironically, for some, the tangible benefits of m-commerce had arrived earlier than anticipated.

Mobile commerce was a vision, not a monolithic entity, and would continue to evolve in the coming years. Innovative forces in the business world built this new channel not knowing all the answers and in many ways let consumers decide what they wanted to make of it. So the clarity in vision and execution would come over time with the maturation of complementing technologies.

Mobile commerce was clearly a vital opportunity for businesses, but first and foremost, it was the consumer who had been empowered with a broader span of choices. In the true spirit of technology democratization, which the Internet pioneered, consumers attained crucial leverage as they were seen as the deciding factor in many of the m-commerce undertakings.

Mobile commerce was in a state of flux, and in the midst of this creative chaos, it carried immense opportunities as well as gigantic challenges. This book has tried to chronicle the amalgam of these opportunities and challenges. Mobile commerce, for instance, was already caught up in the web of legislation and regulation. There could be many new challenges in the m-commerce space. One thing, however, seemed clear: its advancement would intrinsically be linked to innovation in the smartphone and social media realms. A legion of startups was now chasing their dreams to make it big in almost every facet of the m-commerce business. From smartphone vendors to software platform providers and from wireless infrastructure suppliers to content aggregators, all had stakes in the advancement of the m-commerce agenda.

# NOTES

## Prologue

Christina Chaey, "Square Gets In-App Loyalty Cards And A Minor Facelift," *Fast Company*, June 19, 2012.

David Kirkpatrick, "The accidental activist," *Vanity Fair*, April 2011.

Douglas MacMillan, "The iPhone as a Cash Register," *Bloomberg Businessweek*, February 10, 2011.

E. B. Boyd, "How Jack Dorsey's Square Is Accidentally Disrupting The Entire Payment Industry," *Fast Company*, May 23, 2011.

Om Malik, "Jack Dorsey on Square, How It Works & Why It Disrupts," *Gigaom*, December 1, 2009.

Ryan Kim, "Square gets into the loyalty game with digital punch cards," *Gigaom*, June 19, 2012.

Ryan Lawler, "Square's Register and the return of the mom-and-pop shop," *Gigaom*, March 4, 2012.

# Chapter 1

"3G Necessary for M-Commerce Success," *Wireless Week*, October 26, 2001.

Dan Whipple, "Leap of Faith," *Interactive Week*, March 5, 2001.

Jesse Berst, "Don't Be Seduced By the M-Commerce Siren Song," *ZDNet*, April 17, 2000.

Junko Yoshida, "Nokia, not Google, sees itself reshaping the Internet," *EE Times*, February 11, 2008.

Junko Yoshida, "Nokia's naked ambition: Moving beyond cell-phones," *EE Times*, October 23, 2008.

"Looking for the pot of gold," *The Economist*, October 11, 2001.

"Net-enabled cell phones create m-commerce," *Tribune*, October 19, 2000.

"No Quick Cure for Ailing M-commerce Market," *Wireless Week*, October 26, 2001.

"Why mobile is different," *The Economist*, October 11, 2001.

# Chapter 2

Bill Siwicki, "160 Characters or Less," *Internet Retailer*, December 29, 2008.

Bill Siwicki, "E-commerce on the move," *Internet Retailer*, February 28, 2008.

Bill Siwicki, "The smart set," *Internet Retailer*, February 26, 2009.

Brendan Greeley, "One Good Paper: Monopoly Power in Mobile Money," *Bloomberg Businessweek*, March 13, 2013.

Chantal Tode, "Why is SMS not playing a bigger role in brands' marketing efforts?" *Luxury Daily*, July 3, 2012.

Darrell Etherington, "BlackBerry Launches BBM Money Pilot in Indonesia," *TechCrunch*, February 26, 2013.

"Helping Out With a Text," *Newsweek*, October 10, 2010.

"Mobile commerce and SMS history," *Wikipedia*, March 10, 2011.

"Texting the television," *The Economist*, October 17, 2002.

"The joy of text," *The Economist*, September 15, 2001.

Tom Kaneshige, "Haiti Donations: A Turning Point in Mobile Commerce?" *CIO*, February 10, 2010.

# Chapter 3

Arik Hesseldahl, "Apple's iDecade," *Bloomberg Businessweek*, April 26, 2010.

Danielle Kucera, "EBay's Adventures in Brick and Mortar," *Bloomberg Businessweek*, December 23, 2011.

David Murphy, "Making sense of mobile marketing," *The Guardian*, June 6, 2012.

Kathleen Richards, "iTunes App Store: Mobile Revolution?" *Application Development Trends*, August 26, 2008.

Marin Perez, "Mobile Internet To Grow Rapidly By 2010," *InformationWeek*, January 16, 2009.

Olga Kharif, "M-Commerce's Big Moment," *Bloomberg Businessweek*, October 11, 2009.

# Chapter 4

Amir Efrati and Robin Sidel, "Google Sets Role in Mobile Payment," *The Wall Street Journal*, March 28, 2011.

Brad Stone and Olga Kharif, "Pay as You Go with Smartphones," *Bloomberg Businessweek*, July 14, 2011.

Brian X. Chen, "Will the iPhone Become Your iWallet?" *Wired*, August 16, 2010.

Caribou Honig, "It's Apple vs. Google vs. Everyone In The Mobile Payments War," *Forbes*, May 9, 2012.

Caribou Honig, "Tap-To-Pay Smartphones: The Coming Near Field Communications Tsunami," *Forbes*, April 23, 2012.

Dan Rowinski, "NFC In 2012: Time For The Training Wheels," *ReadWriteWeb*, January 5, 2012.

Donald Melanson, "Google Wallet: one year later," *Engadget*, May 26, 2012.

Eric Eldon, "How Green Dot Will Use Loopt To Go After Mobile Payments," *TechCrunch*, March 9, 2012.

Kevin Kelleher, "Apple's Opportunity: Disrupt the Credit Card Business," *ReadWriteWeb*, June 14, 2012.

Kit Eaton, "In The Messy NFC Battle, Consumers Are The Biggest Losers," *Fast Company*, December 14, 2011.

Kit Eaton, "Visa Talks With Apple As Part Of Plan To Push Wireless Payments," *Fast Company*, January 17, 2012.

Jeff Fagel, "Why Passbook could join Ping in the Apple graveyard," *Gigaom*, November 25, 2012.

Jeffrey Glueck, "Don't Call It A Comeback: How Carriers Could Take Back Control of The Mobile Ecosystem," *TechCrunch*, February 25, 2012.

Jessica E. Vascellaro, "Inside Apple's Go-Slow Approach to Mobile Payments," *The Wall Street Journal*, July 6, 2012.

John Brownlee, "Why Apple's iWallet Won't Have Anything To Do With NFC," *Cult of Mac*, May 17, 2012.

Lee Gomez, "Money for the Masses," *MIT Technology Review*, March 27, 2012.

Olga Kharif, "Google Said to Rethink Wallet Strategy Amid Slow Adoption," *Bloomberg Businessweek*, March 21, 2012.

Philip Butta, "The Race For Mobile Payments," *Fast Company*, December 13, 2011.

Phred Dvorak and Stuart Weinberg, "RIM, Carriers Fight Over Digital Wallet," *TheWall Street Journal*, March 18, 2011.

Rip Empson, "Social Passport Marries NFC With Social Media For A New Spin On Mobile Deals," *TechCrunch*, March 8, 2012.

Ryan Kim, "Foursquare Adds Bios To Profile Pages, Evolving As A More Self-Contained Social Network," *Gigaom*, October 20, 2011.

Ryan Kim, "Foursquare and NFC: how the two can help each other," *Gigaom*, February 10, 2012.

Ryan Kim, "Isis recruits big point-of-sale providers for mobile payment push," *Gigaom*, March 5, 2012.

Ryan Kim, "Location-based service Loopt bought for $43.4M by Green Dot Corp," *Gigaom*, March 9, 2012.

Sam Gustin, "Near Field Communication's Big (Money) Moment," *Wired*, May 25, 2011.

Stacey Higginbotham, "Isis in action: It's pretty simple but no replacement wallet," *Gigaom*, October 27, 2012.

# Chapter 5

Adam Turner, "PayPal launches smartphone credit card reader," *Digital Life*, March 19, 2012.

Danielle Kucera, "EBay's PayPal Counts on Its 103 Million Users to Target Groupon," *Bloomberg Businessweek,* December 15, 2011.

Dan Rowinski, "5 Experts Weigh In on the Future of Mobile Money," *ReadWriteWeb*, April 25, 2012.

Dan Rowinski, "As Mobile-Payment Giants Bicker, Startups Step Up," *ReadWriteWeb*, December 5, 2012.

Dan Rowinski, "The World is Not Quite Ready for Mobile Payments, According to MasterCard," *ReadWriteWeb*, May 8, 2012.

David Talbot, "Battle of the Electronic Wallets," *MIT Technology Review*, March 9, 2012.

Dieter Bohn, "The mobile payments mess: no one's winning, but we're all losing," *The Verge*, May 9, 2012.

"Digital payments pose a serious threat to banks," *The Economist*, May 19, 2012.

Jessica Leber, "Beyond Credit Cards: Q&A with Dan Schulman of American Express," *MIT Technology Review*, March 7, 2012.

Michael Della Penna, "How Mobile Payments Will Transform The Shopping Experience," *ReadWriteWeb*, February 12, 2013.

Ryan Kim, "How PayPal Here could lay the hurt on Square and others," *Gigaom*, March 15, 2012.

Ryan Kim, "Juniper: NFC to reach $74 billion in transactions by 2015," *Gigaom*, March 8, 2012.

# Chapter 6

Alyson Shontell, "The $600 Million Social Life Of Foursquare Founder Dennis Crowley," *Business Insider*, February 15, 2012.

Cameron Scott, "Location, location, location fuels mobile apps," *Macworld*, March 14, 2012.

Colleen Taylor, "Foursquare Adds Bios To Profile Pages, Evolving As A More Self-Contained Social Network," *TechCrunch*, March 29, 2012.

Erin Griffith, "Foursquare Redesign: So What if the Check-In is Dead," *Pando Daily*, June 6, 2012.

Ingrid Lunden, "Groupon On A Shopping Spree: Buys Mobile Payment Specialist Kima Labs," *TechCrunch*, February 18, 2012.

Jenna Wortham, "Rather Than Share Your Location, Foursquare Wants to Suggest One," *The New York Times*, June 7, 2012.

Jennifer Couch, "QR Codes for Marketing," *Site Pro News*, July 1, 2012.

Junko Yoshida, "Urgent call to carriers: Deploy enhanced 911," *EE Times*, September 17, 2001.

Meghan Casserly, "Geoloqi, Foursquare's Biggest Threat?" *Forbes*, December 9, 2010.

Rob Woodbridge, "Why Groupon bought Ditto.me," *Unether.tv*, April 26, 2012.

Ryan Kim, "Geoloqi helps location-based services take flight," *Gigaom*, February 23, 2012.

Semil Shah, "Why Location-Based Services Will Create Multiple Winners At The Application Layer," *TechCrunch*, May 8, 2012.

# Chapter 7

Anton Troianovski, "New Wi-Fi Pitch: Tracker," *The Wall Street Journal*, June 18, 2012.

Christopher Mims, "Location-based marketing can increase average order value, frequency, loyalty," *MIT Technology Review*, April 9, 2012.

Dana Mattioli and Miguel Bustillo, "Can Texting Save Stores?" *The Wall Street Journal*, May 8, 2012.

Dan Butcher, "Location-based marketing can increase average order value, frequency, loyalty," *Mobile Marketer*, March 29, 2011.

Jeff Bercovici, "Foursquare Inches Toward Profitability With Visa, MasterCard Deals," *Forbes*, February 26, 2013.

Matt Buchanan, "Foursquare Is The New Yelp," *BuffFeed*, March 11, 2012.

Michael Calore, "How Foursquare Is Forcing Social Networks to Check In or Check Out," *Wired*, March 13, 2012.

Peter Burrows, "Map Apps: The Race to Fill in the Blanks," *Bloomberg Businessweek*, January 12, 2012.

Ryan Kim, "Foursquare hopes new mobile apps make it a go-to local resource," *Gigaom*, June 6, 2012.

Ryan Kim, "Foursquare looks to personalized coupons to generate revenue," *Gigaom*, May 9, 2012.

Sharon Gaudin, "Future smartphone will be assistants, companions," *Computerworld*, September 15, 2010.

# Chapter 8

Dan Butcher, "Location-based marketing can increase average order value, frequency, loyalty," *Mobile Marketer*, March 29, 2011.

Dan Rowinski, "Deep Dive Into Ad Network Behavior on Android," *ReadWriteWeb*, March 19, 2012.

Dirk Smillie, "The App Is The Ad," *Forbes*, March 18, 2010.

*Frank Barbieri,* "Mobile Advertising Is The Baby Huey Of The Media World (And Apple Is Taking The Low Road)," *TechCrunch*, February 18, 2012.

Jason Ankeny, "Ads in apps signal Apple's next mobile revolution," *Fierce Mobile Content*, April 8, 2010.

Nathan Olivarez-Giles, "Motorola's New CEO Could Be Google's Bid to Dominate Mobile Ads," *Wired*, May 24, 2012.

Tom Krazit, "Former iAd executive now playing games with mobile ads," *Gigaom*, March 6, 2012.

Tom MacIsaac, "The Dirty Little Secret About Location-Targeted Mobile Ads," *Verve*, February 19, 2013.

Yukari Iwatani Kane and Emily Steel, "Apple Fights Rival Google on New Turf," *The Wall Street Journal*, April 8, 2010.

# Chapter 9

Antone Gonsalves, "Would You Talk To An Ad On Your Smartphone?" *ReadWriteWeb*, April 9, 2013.

Dan Rowinski, "The Disconnect Between Mobile Advertisers and Consumers," *ReadWriteWeb*, April 5, 2012.

Erica Ogg, "Passbook mobile ticketing expanding to 13 MLB ballparks this season," *Gigaom*, February 26, 2013.

Richard Ting, "Why Mobile Will Dominate the Future of Media and Advertising," *The Atlantic*, June 6, 2012.

Ryan Kim, "Google hopes AdWords + AdMob can solve the mobile monetization gap," *Gigaom*, June 7, 2012.

Sierra Jiminez, "How Google ads reinvented the sales call," *Fortune*, February 7, 2012.

Tom Simonite, "Why No One Likes Mobile Ads and How Companies Hope to Change That," *MIT Technology Review*, March 20, 2013.

# Chapter 10

Dan Rowinski, "Facebook Launches Simple Mobile Payments," *ReadWriteWeb*, June 6, 2012.

Dan Rowinski, "How Facebook's Mobile Strategy Might Create Future Revenue Streams," *ReadWriteWeb*, May 18, 2012.

Douglas MacMillan, "What Facebook Will Get Out of Gift-Giving App Karma," *Bloomberg Businessweek*, May 23, 2012.

Henry Blodget, "Small Twitter Advertiser Calls Some Mobile Ad Results Staggering," *Business Insider*, June 28, 2012.

Josh Constine, "Facebook Did Not Confirm Hyper-Local Mobile Ad Product, But Here's How It Would Target You," *TechCrunch*, June 18, 2012.

Mathew Ingram, "Has Twitter done with mobile ads what Google and Facebook can't?" *Gigaom*, June 29, 2012.

Pascal-Emmanuel Gobry, "Why Twitter Is Poised To Build A Great Mobile Business, *Business Insider*, June 29, 2012.

Peter Vogel, "Why Facebook Is Folding On Credits And Doubling Down On Payments," *TechCrunch*, June 23, 2012.

Robert D. Hof, "How Facebook Slew the Mobile Monster," *MIT Technology Review*, March 6, 2012.

Shayndi Raice, "Facebook to Target Ads Based on App Usage," *The Wall Street Journal*, July 6, 2012.

# Chapter 11

Curtis Staker, "Mobile Commerce Needs New Authentication Schemes," *Forbes*, December 16, 2011.

Theodore Iacobuzio, "Who's Ready For Mobile Payments? The U.S., Canada...And Kenya," *Forbes*, May 7, 2012.

# INDEX

## About The Author

Majeed Ahmad is former Editor-in-Chief of EE Times Asia, a sister publication of EE Times. During his stint as the Editor-in-Chief at Global Sources, a Hong Kong-based publishing house, he also spearheaded magazines relating to electronic components, consumer electronics, and computer, security and telecom products. This is his third book on smartphones. His other two book titles are *Smartphone* and *Nokia's Smartphone Problem*. He has been a technology and trade journalist for more than 17 years.